MW01101732

I Am Existence

Stephen Garvey

Inexpressible Publications

Copyright © 1997 Stephen Garvey

All rights reserved.

Canadian Cataloguing in Publication Data

Garvey, Stephen, 1965-
   I am existence

ISBN 0-9682940-0-6

   1. Philosophy. I. Title.

BD431.G38 1997   191   C97-901110-8

Inexpressible Publications 2035 Panorama Drive North Vancouver BC
V7G 1V2

EPILOGUE

Could I be wrong? Is there something I overlooked? The only possibility is that the *meaning* we give to appearances somehow changes them from meaningless to meaningful though this *cannot* be when *they themselves* are meaningless and regardless of what meaning we give them or not. This is the crucial point because appearances no matter what meaning we give them *never* change from what they really are. We could turn it around and say we are mere appearances too though inexpressible nothingness prevents us from doing that.

So almost *everything* that appears on our minds, regardless of what we think or do, is meaningless. This is not a bleak reality of our existence or a denial of it rather it is simply what really is; and if anything we ought to feel at ease knowing that there *is* meaning, whatever it is, *beyond* our consciousnesses. However, existing our meaning is not that simple because as mentioned our meaning lies outside our minds, *and* we have habituated ourselves to believing that what we perceive is what really is when it is nothing more than appearances of what is not. Nevertheless, existing our meaning is simple if we have the courage and strength to realize the appearances on our minds for what they really are, and we can only do that by realizing inexpressible nothingness in relation to them and them in relation to inexpressible nothingness. By doing this we realize that our meaning is indeed outside our consciousness for the reasons meaningless cannot distinguish meaningless and the meaning of inexpressible nothingness itself is beyond our minds. And what this means is that we *ought* to exist outside of our consciousnesses which we can only do by attaching meaning *only* to appearances themselves that define the limit of our minds or not attaching meaning to anything.

Do we have the strength to exist as the inexpressible meaning of who we are, and beyond this *are* we existing the inexpressible meaning of who we are? We whoever or whatever we are will never know if we are, and by *not* knowing we will know *without* really knowing that we are. Yet, *by* knowing we are or are not we really know that we are *not* existing the unknown something.

Note From The Author

Also available are my writings entitled *The Anti-self* and *Beyond Weakness*. These works are an extension of *I Am Existence* whereby they delve deeper into the nature of our conscious existence. By realizing them we come away existing more from the inexpressible of who we are. Complete the form below and mail along $12.00 for *The Anti-self* or *Beyond Weakness*.

Inexpressible Publications 2035 Panorama Drive North Vancouver BC V7G 1V2

Name:	
Address:	
City:	Postal code:
Province / State:	Phone:

NOTE

After writing for almost a year in solitude, Stephen Garvey completed *I Am Existence* in March 1997. Uncertain of what to do with the work because of his realizations through it, he wrote to eight publishers the three line query:

"I whoever or whatever I am have completed a powerful philosophical work called *I Am Existence*. It is a book for some, and therefore for all, and goes beyond *anything* Friedrich Nietzsche has written."

Five of the publishers replied with rejection letters while the other three did not respond. Determined to go on with his writings, Garvey began writing the *The Anti-self* in April 1997 and completed it in June 1997. Instead of querying publishers, from July to September 1997 he went on to write another work entitled *Beyond Weakness*. Mid-way through it, he wrote twelve publishers about the three works and even travelled to New York to meet some; and yet again he was rejected in the form of rejection letters and no responses.

It was at this point, having been rejected by eighteen publishers, Garvey made the decision to start Inexpressible Publications, and thereby make his writings available to the public.

CONTENTS

PART TWO: WITHIN THE SURRENDER

FREEDOM FANTASY

NEEDS DECEPTION

EXISTENCE

EPILOGUE

FOR SOME AND THEREFORE FOR ALL

FOREWARD

What do we know and why do we know it; and can we go further and ask ourselves why do we believe to know anything including to know itself?

If there is no such thing as knowledge except for what we imagine, we may wonder why we plan and organize our existence as though there is. Does this mean we are prepared to exist according to the fabricated order of reason even though it may be only imaginary?

As long as we exist from our minds we ought not be afraid to ask why and how do we. Though to answer these we must examine our root values and beliefs on our minds. Yet, to do this we must overcome the ones blocking us from doing so.

Even if we uncover our root values we need other ones to examine them unless we hold our values static and move back and forth between them except there will always be the unknown.

Could there be something else we are overlooking that will explain why we do and think the things we do? The force behind this is that there appears to be something questionable about our conscious existence since we must attach to our minds and then exist instead of just existing who or what we are. For this reason there must be an explanation for what is questionable unless the explanation is part of what is questionable. Although this may not be the case because we are dealing with who or what we are and our minds.

Join myself and the solitaire in a journey through our minds to find out what we really value and believe, if anything at all, and why. Just maybe we will discover why we attach meaning to our minds themselves and what it means to do so. Could there not be a more important task because our beliefs and values determine why and how we exist!

Stephen Garvey

September 7 1997
Deep Cove, British Columbia

PART ONE: SURRENDER TO REALITY

SURRENDER TO HUMAN NATURE

What Do Candles Mean?

I'm watching this candle. It's fascinating. The flame is erect and bright. Wait. Now it's flickering, and there is less brightness. Again it is erect and bright. I feel warmth. It is beginning to lean to one side. The flame is leaning further; now it moves back. It is erect, but half its size. Brightness and warmth are diminished. The flame is calm. It is not doing anything. Hold on. It is growing. There is a slight flicker. The flicker is increasing. The flame swipes at one side. The flicker is intensifying. Again the flame swipes. It is fluttering; it is growing; it is lashing from side to side. The flame is still growing. The movements are frantic. And now! It is tiny. Wax is dripping down the side of the candle. Do you sense a similarity? Could our glorified, esteemed, and ambiguous emotions be no different from the mere flickers and movements of a flame? They are! We take a step back and assess the paradox, and we see the *flab* of mediocrity. There is no flame without the candle and match. There is no candle or match without a person creating the candle and match. There is no flame without a person striking the match. The flame does not move without external forces like a breeze. Hence, the flame and its movements are contingent not on itself, but on things *outside* of it. The flame is part of a larger connection of beings. It is not an end. It is an end result. And it is only an end result if we perceive it as that. We could perceive *beyond*. What about our emotions? Are they magical, mystical, and even divine occurrences from *being* human beings or are they also part of a larger connection between beings? They are inventions and even fabrications. We must press forward! They are contingent on our *consciousness* which is created from words and rules. People invent the rules and words. The words form ideas which correspond to, among other things, our so-called emotions. Our emotions are contingent on the circularity of the rules and words which form them. They move not from themselves, but external forces like *mediocrity*. Similar to the flame they have no independent existence. They are end

15

results of an invention called consciousness. I blow out the flame. There is the sun. I erase our consciousness. There is existence.

Oh the centuries of human *waste*. The labour, the effort of almost endless minds for what? To codify and capture our prized, our illusory, our non-existent emotions? Our literature, our plays, our relationships, our existence denounced meaningless! Our customs, our cultures rendered void. Their only value being relics, memories of the great lie: our belief in love. There is *no* love. There is sickness of the mind, sickness of being. There are the weak, the gregarious. There are the strong, the eliminators of weakness. We are few, but we rumble. We rumble the giant promoter of emotions, the *giant* exploiter of weakness. We rumble Shakespeare and all his works! They are the entertainment of lies, the lies of entertainment. We are earthquakes. We rumble under the feet of Romeo and Juliet, the feet of the dishonest, the feet of the weak. "Earn your existence!" we demand, we rumble from the depths of us. The two of them are gone because they were never here. What they stand for is *fantasy* just like compassion, pity, happiness, joy, sadness, rage, anger, and hatred, and others and others. Wait. We smell something. It is one of the impersonators of human nature. It is the pungent draft that has moved the flame, that has infected and influenced our minds and actions. It is the *morality* of happy and sad, love and hatred, *and* good and bad. It is not alone. There is *technology* the spring to mediocrity. *Mediocrity* the spring to more mediocrity. They are all in on it. And the good sheep have herded and divided. They have distractions. They have excuses. They have emotions. "He hates me." "We are in love." "I am sorry." "They despise him." "She is sad." "You are mean." "He is jealous." "I am happy." "We pity them." The sheep are hidden from themselves in their manufactured minds. And they have things to do and talk about. They have things to watch and dream about. The webs of the marketplace are sticky. The spiders are near. It is to be civilized.

The stage has been set. It is the web. We are all actors. We act to get what we want. We cry. We laugh. We shout. We love. Some of us believe it is real. Some of us do it more than others. Some of us even act out our acts. And we praise them for it. We praise them for acting out our lies. It is all a disguise. To act is to disguise. We are disguising the hardness of existence. And yet there is nothing to hide. We are soft. We are weak. Sure we exploit weakness, but we don't eliminate it. We are weakness exploiting weakness. We are spiders without the bite. We are insects without the sense to avoid webs. We call it progress. Progress to get technology to do our work for us. Progress to be able to act out our manufactured fantasies. We are in the flab! Listen to the laughs. Watch the smiles. Smell the pity. Get beneath them, and you'll see existence lurking. It is withered. It is hungry. It is tired of the lies. The weaker we get the closer we are to existence! It is not a paradox. It is hard reality. 'Enough!' is the demand from within. What are we going to do? Existence can't be contained inside us. We can't control it. And even mediocrity has a limit for itself. It is prompting us to strike at itself. Existence is driving us to strike at mediocrity, to strike at the weakness of others, and even at ourselves. It is driving us to preserve ourselves, to preserve the species. The stage is turning into existence. The actors are taking off their masks. There are no curtains to draw. There is no place to hide. The demand is waiting. The strong have begun their ascent. I smother the flame. It is light for some. I expose *it* in all of us.

I am existence!

What Do Secluded Cabins Mean?

Our fear of the monsters! Our tolerance of the monsters! For what? Look at them. The beached masses of mediocrity. They are taking up space. They are spreading weakness. They have razor like claws, and they can't use them. They depend on the masses for existence. The all-powerful monsters depend on the herds. They depend on beings who have no faith in themselves. They depend on beings who do not want to earn existence. And many of them can't. These are not monsters. They are breeding grounds for weakness. They are collections of weakness that have been tolerated for too long. They are the great mighty herds. Herds that do not move. Herds that would rather not exist than exist! When will the earthquakes rumble? When will the masses erupt from inside? When will the disgust of mediocrity become unbearable? It is coming. Nobody is *beyond* accountability. And yet we look down from a mountain at the mass of sickly excess covered by swallow air. We hear its uneven breath and feeble whines. We watch its paw scratch against its sagging flesh. We smell its stench. I turn away. I cling to mountain air and the scent from trees growing up all around us. I feel the vitality of moss under our feet. Moss that has *earned* its existence. Moss that is striving for more existence. I hear the buzz of mosquitoes. I watch leaves flutter from a slight breeze. Come. We move further into the mountains of purity. We do not forget. We take cover in the demand. We strengthen through our own weakness.

'Don't go! There's nothing to see or do,' is the advice on our minds.

Existence rumbles from inside me. I am alone. The weak have left themselves behind. Some have returned to the herd. Others were left at a cliff. They gaped at the glowing sun lowering below the vast blue sky with long, golden orange clouds drifting and spreading across the vast sky, worn mountains with a sharpness to them resting firm and with pride, and tiny, white crested waves appearing and disappearing like the flash of dolphins while hearing the faint rhythmic crash of the tide and noticing the determined flow of migrating geese. They marveled at the oneness of the view. "Nothing is out of place," one of them remarked. The weak do not consider themselves. They do not rumble. And they are forgetful. Those at the cliff will *return* at the end of sunset. Are you with them?

My disgust has its grip on me. And yet I am on my *own* cliff. It is jagged. There is no view. I scale down into an abyss. I *will* fall. I shake off my disgust. There is an idea of *courage*. I grab onto it. I lower myself into the abyss. I lower myself onto the idea of *honesty*. It is my weapon. It is my explosives. I breath in the idea of *patience*. I am armed. The hunt has begun. I prey on the weakness of my mind. There is a mist. There is no trail. The way down is rocky and steep. There are faint voices from below. I past memories of self-doubt and images of the weak. 'I could go back,' passes on my mind. The thunder of *law* claps from below. I slip on the idea of guilt. Honesty is my support. Patience is my aim. Courage is my sledgehammer. Strike! I continue down. My legs ache. They wobble. What is it? I know what it is. I will fall into darkness. There is *no* abyss. I have been fooled. Morality where are you?! I think you out. The idea of science. The idea of manufactured good. Scientists the *great* defeatists. The devisors of how *not* to exist. The fearful hidden behind the procedures and results of isolated reason. What is it that guides them? Is it science's fundamental equation, one plus one equals two? No! They know. In existence there is no such thing as two identical units. It is only on our minds. What guides them is the idea of good. The illusory good of the mind. They are the priests of science who have faith in reason rather than God. They are anti-existence. Cowards are them. They do not seek or want accountable. They want the species to de-exist. They do not believe in themselves. They have *contempt* for the species and existence. They have surrendered to weakness of mind. Morality you chameleon! First religion and now science! I now know. You are the disease of existence. You are the explosive. Our minds are time bombs. The demand of existence is on us. We are being accounted. I defuse my mind.

Solitude is the cracker. Morality is the nut. Existence is the force. Yet who has the strength to enter our mind dumps? Who has the courage to confront the lie of morality? It is our test. We have to earn the honesty of solitude. A state where there is nothing to hide behind. A state where our thoughts, our ideas are exposed. It is a self-interrogation of our minds. It makes the weak tremble. "No don't do it!" they cry out. They know. They ridicule and torment the solitaires, loners, recluses! They label them as madmen, lunatics, social outcasts! They even create zones of settlement to keep them with the weak and out of secluded cabins. It is the great condemnation of the strong. It is the *great* lie of our existence. It is the demand testing the strong.

Solitude is earned. We have to be worthy. It is the highest state of being. It is the closest thing to being one. It is an affirmation of who we are. It is beings seeking their *own* way and attempting to be themselves. It is to say Yes to existence and Yes to being! Morality cannot co-exist in solitude. It cracks in solitude. And yet the weak have invented a way. They have created ascetics to further tarnish the sacredness of solitude. And the weak use morality and technology to lead and take them into it. Though there is *more* to solitude than just being in it. It is a state of being. It is an inner need to become closer to who we are. It is not praying, repenting, and chanting what we think we want to be or what we believe. It is not hiking or sightseeing. Solitude is exposing the *demand* to our minds. It does not require faith in God. It does not require faith in ourselves. Solitude requires knowing. It is the courageous, the strong striving to strengthen through their own weakness. It is an affirmation of existence. It is to act, to say Yes! I want, I *will* be myself. I will exist!

I am existence!

What Do Raised Huts Mean?

"It's just a raised hut. A hut on stilts. There is nothing more to it," the weak cry out. I explode through their attempts to redirect my instinct. I sense strength, and through the strength there is weakness. I am not looking at a hut. I am looking at a *symbol* of our earned strength. Strength comes from weakness. Animals were in our food which is an extension of us. It is our weakness. Those tree stomps and the tree trunks supporting the hut are the remains of the weakness we used to strengthen. We ourselves strengthened by becoming more self-sufficient. We did not blame the animals. There is no poison bait or traps, nor is there a barbed wire fence. We recognized our own weakness, and dealt with it through our *own* means. Our instinct identified the weakness as us. Our reason estimated the animals' strength, and created the idea for a raised hut. Our instinct consented to it. We acted it out. Could this be an example of human nature, an example of the nature of all beings?! Don't let us fool ourselves. It is subtle, ever so subtle. It is *not* about conformity or obedience to our minds, or blaming others for our difficulties; nor is it about relying on unnatural technology to avoid facing weakness in ourselves. It is about sensing and responding to weakness. It is an unconscious recognition of our relation to the entirety of existence.

Existence ebbs and flows, creates and destroys, and strengthens and weakens within different intensities of itself. There is no center point. Everything is condition on everything else in relation to their strength. Everything exists within the cycles of existence. The cycles are infinite. We are part of them. There is no human nature. There is movement to greater strength. It is the nature of existence. We the creators of the

20

raised hut are part of it. We are mere parts of the universal movement to strength. Our every action no matter how subtle results in cycles which spin off into existence while we enter other cycles from all around us. The blade of grass which we have just stepped on. The air we are breathing. The chipmunk which has nibbled at our food. The trees we cut down to build the hut. All these and endless others spin off from endless other cycles and into endless other ones. The blade of grass absorbing more nutrients from the soil. Nearby chipmunks having more food. Plants flourishing around the tree stomps. A spider spinning its web between the hut and one of the tree trunks supporting it. And there are endless other cycles in between them and after, and after. It is the infinity of existence. The infinity of the constant flux between weakness and strength, strength and greater strength, greater strength and greater strength still.... The complexity of the interaction between beings within the endless cycles, I am weakness, I am strength, I eliminate weakness, the complexity of the interactions between cycles within the cycle, we are weakness, we are strength, we eliminate weakness.... It is all happening at once and continuously from limitless sides. It is an infinite accountability of all beings. It is a universal movement upward! A will of all beings to exist. An ascent by and from all beings to the finer and purer cycles of existence. A state where the free move with and amongst the free. A state where there is an unconsciousness existence of strength. A state where existence and non-existence blend into one. The raised hut and the cycles that brought it into being are part of the ascent. And so are these words and so our we.

The essence of the cycle, the essence of the cycles, the essence of all beings is existence. It is the impartial drive to strengthen through weakness. There is no end or beginning. The drive to strength, the movement to purity is all there is. It is endless and constant. There are no favourites. The past, the future have meaning only because they influence the fleeting moment of existence. The moment stands alone. There are no excuses. There are no testimonies. Evidence is not weighed in scales of morality. There is one evidence: strength or weakness. It is the evidence of the moment. There are no judges and sentences. There is the point of intersection between being and non-being. The flash of our instinct, the impulse of our being from the sparkle of existence which tells us where weakness lies. It is a moment of truth, a moment of preservation and continuance of all beings. There is no courtesy, attachments, or obligations. It is an impulse of purity from the depths of us. It is our guide from purity to purity. And how can it be otherwise! Purity has to be earned. There is no wavering. Strength through weakness is the meaning of our instinct, our existence. There is no other meaning. There is no other meaning to our actions. The demand shines from within. And it is in this moment of intersection and infinite others which lights the uncompleted path to freedom. It is our account of mediocrity which moves us through weakness and onto untrodden ground. It is our courage and honesty which ascends us to the purest state of existence: the end of weakness within the oneness of mortality and strength. I am existence!

What Do Hunting Hats Mean?

We put on hunting hats, and we are hunters. We take off the hunting hats. What are we? I explode with laughter through the manufactured roles of morality. I ascend above the self-serving classifications of reason. I look down and cringe at human beings struggling with one another over things they are not, over things they will never be. It is the compromise, the decadence of morality. It is the fabricated division between good and bad. Morality can't bear us being warriors and yet the state makes exceptions! It is the crack of weakness, the division of good itself into good and bad, into nothingness. How convenient for those who are the authorities on what is good. They can justify anything as moral! And the herd comes into being because they believe these arbitrators of lies. I strike down on the fraud, the weakness. I don't arbitrate anything because there is nothing, but lies to arbitrate. I act from instinct. Be warned moralists you will be accounted. Your fabrications already point back to you. You cannot cover up the smell of dishonesty. We the strong are outside the web of your ideas. We are not fooled, and we cannot be stopped. It is the demand of existence. We are the demand. Earned strength is our purpose. We are beginning to always wear our hunting hats. There will be a time when we will not need them.

The time is not for a war. War is a conception that can only come from morality. The time is for an eruption of existence from within the species. And there is a lot of weakness to be accounted for.

"Why does it matter?" ask the moralists. "We can all exist together. We can work together. A collective can produce more than individuals."

It is the *cry* of the herd. They reduce the meaning of existence to a discussion of ideas. Their voice echoes their great numbers and rings with morality. They cling to our basest level of existence: meeting our material needs. There is no consideration of freedom. There is no will to strengthen. Why would they? They are not interested in earning their existence. They are interested in getting by, and with the least effort. They have used the weakness of morality to raise themselves up. It was their decision. And now there is no more morality to hold onto! And yet they still cling. I can't bear the breathers of anti-existence. I don't want any part of it. I am a hunter. Weakness is my prey. Instinct is my guide. There is no acting. There are no disguises. And still the weak clutch to their only defense: to not exist. They cease to be neither weakness nor strength. We are not deceived. We do not harm them. It is not our purpose to harm for the sake of harming. Though we will strike when the weak *show* their faces. We will strike the weak in our area of existence just as we are struck ourselves. It is to be part of the infinite accountability of existence. There are no grudges or revenge. There is the endless movement to purity. So weak! you can fall at our feet and play dead. You can turn your cheek to one side and the other. You can quote your proverbs. You can mention your theories. You can list your facts. We are not fooled. Instinct is our guide. It does not lie!

The dynamic of existence is the *eternal* hunt and hunted. It is the force behind the ebbs and flows, creations and destructions, and strengths and weaknesses of existence. We are the hunters and the hunted. There is no choice. There are no pauses. The dynamic is constant within the variability of our strengths and weaknesses. It is not a barbaric release of energy rather it is a force asking us to earn our existence. We are not expected to be anybody who we are not. It is the opposite! The dynamic demands and ensures that we be ourselves. It is only by being ourselves that we will ensure our own existence. The hunters of weakness and the hunted weakness are all around us, and we are both of them at the same time. Our every movement, breath, and thought is condition on the weakness of something else, and that is the same for every being. There is a constant demand on weakness. We are in the fire of eternal accountability. Strength is feeding off weakness within infinite variations and transformations of the strengths and weaknesses themselves. There are no escapes. Weakness will result in more weakness. Strength will eventually succumb to weakness. Weakness pretending to be non-existent will be eliminated by strength and weakness. There is no where to hide. The more we hunt the more we are sought by the hunted. The less we hunt the more we need to hunt. It is the test of all tests, and it does not end! We are forced to act or perish. By acting we are strengthened through the weakness of something else. By perishing we are returned in another form. There is no giving up. We cannot fight existence. The fire is eternal, and we are eternal parts of it! We can burst into flames or delay the inevitable. In either case we *will* return. There is a call from within and all around. It is the call to surrender. It is from all of us. It is the silent call to exist! to be ourselves through weakness. I am existence!

What Do Campfires Mean?

It is the gathering of the weak! We can hear their tales, stories, songs of lies amidst the crackle of the campfire. It is the ghost of morality. It has come to relieve them of their boredom. It has come to comfort them in their sleepy existence. They look into the fire and see images of the struggle between good and bad. "It's spooky. I'm scared," they whisper and cry to one another. They fantasize about the fire itself as though there is something mystical about strength through weakness! And then it is forgotten when they toast their squares of white, sugary gob. Around and within the weak the hunters and hunted lurk. They huddle closer from a cool midnight wind. They edge away from the intense heat of the fire. Darkness looms around them. They become tired. Morality through science and religion looses its grip and scent on the prey. Beneath the veil of dishonesty, the warmth from blankets, and within their feeble bodies existence moves! We need each other is the unanimous, and yet silent agreement of the weak. We need each other to have meaning, to have existence. It is the weak exploiting and existing off the weakness of themselves and others. They are not there to sing and stuff themselves. They are there for one and only one reason: there is weakness. And it is through the weakness of each other that they become more strengths than they would be otherwise. Oh, but morality has feasted on their minds! Nature through mosquitoes and the slaps of a cool wind has taken its share. And they have pulled each other down through exploitation of each others' weakness disguised as relationships and friendships. Even though they all think it was *only* themselves who made others accountable. It is the collective dishonesty and vanity of the weak. We all have to exist. And this is their way.

We the strong move towards the campfire. It is in the fire that we see and feel the strength and purity of the will to exist. We are drawn to the symbol, the affirmation of strength through weakness. We are drawn to the dynamic between strength and weakness. We are drawn to the meaning of existence. We peer into it. The flames of the fire are feeding off the wood and air. Smoke and debris rise and burst out of the fire. They are on their way to nourish plants and other beings. Inside the fire insects which have rested in the wood are now adding to the smoke. We ourselves are cold. We collect more wood. We place it in the fire. A cold wind passes between us and challenges the fire. It responds by feeding more off the wood, and thereby comes closer to its return. Weakness is its only means for continuance, for end, and for return. The strength of the fire alone has *no* meaning. Strength alone has no meaning. It is only *through* weakness that it comes into being. It is only through weakness that anything comes into being and sustains itself. And it is only by coming into being that anything else is sustained. It is the endless dynamic, the eternal pulse of existence.

We the strong stand around the blaze defiant to the pulse of existence. There is an unspoken honesty between us. We do not feed off the weakness of each other. We feed off our strengths. We have surrendered to existence, and therefore to each other. There is precision in our elimination of weakness. There is no hesitation. There are no songs. Our minds are clear. We have become more hunters than the hunted. We have earned our ascent. It is to breath on a higher state of existence. A state where the strong elevate each other to higher levels of being. A state where there is mutual respect and recognition of each others' strength. It is to bask in each others' shine. There is contentment amongst us. And yet our contentment is the barrier to the final ascent! It is our last and most formidable test. It is to rise through the weakness of each other. It is make our own path. It is to ascend alone, to ascend into the existence of no weakness. It is to be no longer seen.

There is a lone fire. It is the fire of eternal accountability. In the tip of its flame *the solitaire* meditates. There are tears in his eyes. He knows how he has come to be who he is. He knows it is weakness that is the ultimate determinate of existence! He feels his powerlessness, his dependency on weakness. There is something else. He knows the time for purity has not come. There is no hiding from it. The demand rumbles inside him. It is a call to exist, to be part of the eternal movement to purity.

He wipes the tears from his face and takes a breath. 'There is weakness to be accounted for!' flashes on his mind from the depths of him. He begins his decent.

The solitaire meets up with the strong whom he had left.

"We have not earned it," he says.

They move closer to him.

"As long as there is weakness we have not earned it," continues the solitaire. He looks at each of them. "There is no higher existence as long as there is weakness. It is strength through weakness until there is no more. That is our earned end and beginning!"

The strong mutter to themselves as they follow him down.

One of them asks him, "if there is more weakness does that mean we will become stronger than if there was less?"

The solitaire pauses. "There are no shortcuts to earning existence. There is no greater individual strength. We all strengthen through weakness. The less weakness there is the more strength there is. The more weakness there is the less strength there is. The end is to eliminate all weakness. It is to earn the purest existence, an existence without weakness. That is the strength we earn. There is *no* higher being. There is freedom in purity of existence."

"When will we know?" asks one of the strong.

"Instinct," the solitaire replies.
I am existence!

SURRENDER TO MORTALITY

What Do Graves Mean?

In the glowing coals of the fire the solitaire meditates. He explores human consciousness not for our weakness. He explores it for the *foundations* of our weakness. History has no meaning to him. Guiding ideas are his prey. He is alone. Resting his chin on his hand, he looks up at the serenity of the flame. Its clarity and purity. Its even distribution of heat. He returns to the coarse glow of the coals. There are no tears. His eyes radiate disgust for the species.

'There is a constancy to all states,' flashes on his mind. 'They are all founded and exist on the premise that there is life and death.' His eyes are closed. He imagines generations, races, entire civilizations chained by and to the ideas of happy and sad, good and bad, and life and death. He imagines the masses existing in conformity for what they believe is and in fear of what is to come. 'It is the great antitheses, the great divisions of our existence! Yet there are no divisions. There is no end,' he reflects to himself. 'There is becoming. There are different states of being. There is eternal accountability.'

'Nothing itself,' he continues, 'is created or destroyed. And nothing is unaccountable. We ourselves will always exist.'

'If there is no end there is no death. If there is no death there is no life. There is existence!' he reflects.

'We respect the eerie place of the dead. We pay respect to the dead and let them rest in peace! And we exist knowing our own end is to come. It is all an illusion. We have been fooled. I split life and death in two. And there is *mortality*. It is the bane of our existence, the thing everybody would like to forget. Upon hearing it we feel disgraceful, inferior, unclean. We turn and lower our heads. And yet by attaching to life and death we attach to mortality. We attach to a pronouncement against our existence, a pronouncement that denies us any hope. And there is no hope. We can't prevent our deaths. So we try to forget and deny them. We are trapped by the *mortality illusion*.'

The solitaire hears the voices of the weak. He looks over at them standing together.

28

"Why did he have to bring that up?" "He's morbid!" "I despise him." "He's sick," they say to each other.

'It is a test. My existence, my weakness is being challenged. I am being made accountable,' passes on the solitaire's mind. He turns away.

'We have been misguided by our teachers and leaders. We have succumbed to weakness of mind,' he thinks to himself. 'Shakespeare the authority on existence has no will of truth. He writes about what people want to hear. He writes about life and death amidst goblins, witches, spirits, and devils. And when he has an opportunity to confront non-truth he backs away. At the grave of Ophelia he does not have Hamlet confront death. No! Hamlet realizes through the skulls lying about him that we all, even the likes of Alexander the Great, end in death. Hamlet retreats from the *illusion* of death and into life. He becomes like Shakespeare himself a pagan. I challenge the naive, weak thoughts of Shakespeare. I expose his pride and contempt for truth. He is not the only one. Dickens writes that we can't take our money with us, but does not inquire further. And except for Heraclitus, Nietzsche, and a few others there are no philosophers or writers who go *beyond* life and death.'

'Our leaders, our states reflect the ideas of our teachers. In almost all states there are ceremonies and memorials for the dead lost in wars and deceased Heads of States. In communities there are graveyards. We are surrounded by death. It is the great reminder and fear! that we are *mortal*. It is a check on our existence. It is a means of social control. It is a call to be pagans! We don't confront death. We accept it. It becomes the basis for our existence. And the meaning of our existence comes down to living because if it doesn't we will die sooner than we would otherwise.'

"He's gone mad!" "He's gone mad!" "He's gone mad!" the weak cry out.

The strong hear the cries. They see the solitaire.

"What has thou thought to cause such a response?" one of them asks him.

"Our weakness is not the pagan and mortal non-truths. Our weakness is that we *believe* them," he replies. "And the reason we believe them is because we overvalue ourselves and the world, and our lives in it. We

29

don't want to know that we are tiny parts of a vast, eternal state of being. We don't want to except that our history, politics, culture have almost no meaning in existence. Instead we attach to them and ourselves as if there is a heightened thing called life! And we create time to give it meaning. We are defeatists. We don't exist in a state of eternal becoming. No! We believe there is a definite end. We are stagnant. There is no movement to greater freedom and purity. There is self-indulgence. It is to be in an existence inverse to existence itself. It is to be trapped between the nothingness of the world and the mortality illusion."

The strong wait for more. Behind them the voice of the weak echoes, "he's a madman!" "It's from his childhood." "Didn't you know his parents are to blame?"

"The use of mortality as a means for social control is increasing," the solitaire continues. "Though we are becoming less surrounded by symbols and memorials of death our lives are becoming more guided by our deaths. The trap is closing on itself. We are descending into nothingness of our minds. It is to be caught in empty ideas which are contingent on others. Our lives have become so meaningless that death itself has lost meaning. And the world has become so meaningless that it cannot co-exist with death. Instead it *exploits* death. Life and death are becoming one. We are moving closer to existence!"

I am existence!

What Do Heavens Mean?

"Leave me to my thoughts. The time has not come. Go! *Account* for weakness," the solitaire says to the strong.

"It is a yea for existence," one of them responds.

They turn and begin their roam of the glowing coals.

A few of them stay behind and listen.

"The secret to finding weakness is to look for it in and around the weakest," the solitaire says to them. "It is the weak through the weakest. The weak through the weak or through the strong requires too much effort."

"Go and earn your existence!" he then demands

They leave and begin their roam.

'The mortality illusion is the *most* widespread weakness of the species,' the solitaire reflects to himself.

'It is a trough for the weak. I question the religious for their dishonesty, for their cowardliness, for their exploitation of our weakness. It is the prophets and Jewish priests who were the first to capitalize on the mortality illusion. They did not care about the species. They looked upon it with contempt. They wanted to control it for their own gain. And they did for hundreds and hundreds of years, and even now there are weak still under their control and the control of others' through Christianity and other religions. I account the religious. They are not strong. They feed off weakness not to eliminate it. They feed off weakness to create more of it!'

'From out of our belief in mortality the religious created the morality illusion and most important the immortality illusion. It is ingenious. They devised a way for the species to transcend death. They called it immortality: an existence without death. And through morality they established the conditions to be met for it. They countered paganism through the *division* of good and bad, and the rewards and punishments of eternal afterlives. In other words, they expanded on our fear of death and set up rules for a way out. We believed and followed them, and thereby detached ourselves further from existence. They took control over the species.'

'The key to their fabrication is the immortality illusion. Without that they would not be able to counter paganism. However, it is condition on mortality, and as we know mortality is an illusion, a weakness. Their system of ideas is founded on weakness. When they devised it they must have been fooled by mortality as much as anybody else. They must have been ignorant of the true nature of existence! It is the single weakness in their theories: there has to be death. Without death immortality ceases to have meaning. Without death the reasons to abide by morality do not have meaning. Without death their religious theories disappear into nothingness, and so does paganism which is *also* based on offsetting mortality.'

'For those doubters I scrutinize the immortality illusion on its own. To be immortal is to no longer be a being. It is to exist outside existence itself. It is to have no physical body or mind. There is no accountability.

WHAT DO SKIN CREAMS MEAN?

There are no wants, desires, needs, or purposes. There is an eternal state of *no* movement or change. It is to be frozen in an eternal state of non-existence! The source of immortality is our *minds*. It came from our minds and can only exist on them. In existence it is not even eternal nothingness. It is nothingness.'

'However, the religious claim that immortality is a reward for our faith in the moral code of religion. And they even claim that there are different states of nothingness: heaven and hell or good nothingness and bad nothingness. Hence, morality is a constant check on us. If we are bad we do not go to heaven, and if we are bad in heaven we go to hell. It is to be in the circle of good and bad *in* either mortality or immortality. Their ideas become even more absurd when they claim that immortal nothings in hell are punished through mortal infliction! To be immortal is to be immortal. And yet they assert the bad can be both immortal and mortal.'

'By the mere fact that we die we become immortal. We transcend our bodies and the eternal accountability, and say no to existence *without* any of our doing. We de-exist in state of nothingness.'

'In our minds I eliminate mortality, and therefore the fabrications of religion. I account the religious for the weakness of their own minds, and also the weak for believing they could avoid the demand of existence. There is no hiding. The strong there's our weakness. Do you know? Do you know for yourselves?'

I am existence!

What Do Skin Creams Mean?

The solitaire holds his meditation on the trough of mortality. 'There is another one!' flashes on his mind. He rests his hand against his chin in a moment of consternation. 'The strong must be here,' he thinks to himself. 'They must be warned!'

He looks around and into the stares of the weak. A feeling of disgust erupts from inside him. 'The weaknesses, the distractions are ubiquitous,' he reflects. He turns around.

'I hold the reins! I conserve energy,' flashes on his mind. 'I build the fire. I shield the fire. I explode from the fire.'

SURRENDER TO MORTALITY

"Be true, be true thy strong. Move with thy honesty and courage. Strike with thy instinct," he says to himself. 'Thou returns. Thou returns to the trough. I go alone,' passes on his mind.

'Science I yank you out of it. Wipe your face. You are a disgrace! Your belly is sagging from your idleness. Your mind is slow to respond from its endless rows and columns of facts. And it's you who takes the meaning out of life. It is you who attempts to make life efficient. It is you who attempts to structure life!'

'Beyond all your tests, controls, experiments, facts, theories, laws, and hypotheses what are you? What guides you? What do you amount to? Paganism has returned. Science is nothing more than organized paganism through the use of reason. The basis for its existence is life and death. Its purpose is to postpone our deaths, and improve our lives through an understanding of the forces behind life. However, since there is no mortality, science has almost no meaning. It is limited to the illusory cycles of life and death instead of the endlessness of existence. Whatever gains it does make are meaningless in existence. Paganism has no role or place in existence. In other words, our purpose is not sensual and material pleasure in consecutive life spans. Our purpose is to strengthen the species through individual accountability.'

'However, science has even failed in improving our lives. What its scientists do not and will not understand is that meaning comes from not just doing things, but creating, experiencing, and doing things for ourselves. Instead they organize and control the framework of our lives. And they pride themselves on being authorities on knowledge. They do not celebrate life. There is no spontaneity. There is no thrill in being alive. There is methodical synthesizing of facts contingent on the mortality illusion. They do not act. Scientists observe and process. They try to understand how things work without knowing the basis for them or the meaning of them. They note and analyze the illusion of life and death, and by doing that they consider themselves experts on it. They are beings who believe they have traveled far and seen lots without having left the place they started. They are beings who have chosen to exist in the illusions of their minds rather than existence. These are the authorities on life and death.'

The solitaire pauses. He senses a frontier never before tread upon.

33

WHAT DO SKIN CREAMS MEAN?

Something is holding him back.

'I can't conceptualize it,' passes on his mind.

He knows to step forward is to never return as is. He feels the fear of others. He senses he is alone.

'It is to go against direction of the species. It is to face ridicule and hatred. It is to be more lonely than I have ever felt,' he reflects.

'Science itself is condition on weakness,' flashes on his mind. 'It intertwines itself with the morality and mortality illusions. It depends on the weakness of our minds. It has no basis for existence in itself. It thrives off weakness for its existence on our minds. It is not an end. Science is weakness from weakness. It exists in opposition to existence. It contributes to our weakness. It does not make us stronger. No! Science counters the eternal accountability. It buffers and shields us from the demand. We are denied the means to strengthen! We do not rely on ourselves. We rely on medicine, engineering, physics, biology, chemistry, and others. We do not earn our existence. We depend on the clergy of scientists. And science knows that to control our environment is to almost perfect its work. That is its end. To create a controlled environment where everything and everybody will be accounted for, where most of its laws and theories can have meaning. Science is not anti-existence. It is a *destroyer* of existence. It is at war with our only means to freedom and purity. There is no acceptance of existence or surrender to it. Science knows that it cannot co-exist with existence. It needs to replace existence and therefore ourselves to ensure its survival. It needs to establish reasoned order.'

'The basis for it is our subservience through our environment and minds. To control our own environment is to control its effect on our minds. To eliminate the weakness of our minds through instinctual deconstruction is to eliminate science. We would be left with common sense.'

'I am alone. I don't how to proceed,' passes on his mind. 'I can't go back. I don't know my way.'

'Everything has shifted to inside. There is no excess on our minds. We are responsible, accountable for ourselves. We determine our own existence. There is no outside intrusion or controls. There are no skin creams to prevent aging. We are cautious and respectful of ourselves. We

34

determine the limits of our own actions. The weak are eliminated from their own doing. The strong strengthen themselves.'

'Instinct is the spring to our actions. We view our minds with skepticism. They are kept simple and strong. There are no experiments. There are no facts. There are no subjects. There are ideas through instinct. We think through sense. We act through thoughts. We think through sense.... It is to be moving, flowing in existence. There are no categories. There are no divisions. Our minds, our beings are one with existence.'

'We are pulses of strength through weakness. We strike weakness. We sacrifice ourselves to eliminate it. The dance of existence does not stop. It is inside and all around. We move with lightness and grace. We shine with honesty. We ascend through weakness. We return again. We ascend....'

'Courage,' the solitaire says to himself. 'Courage to persevere!'
I am existence!

What Do Metal Bars Mean?

'Do I have the courage? I am wavering. I am afraid of alienation. And yet I sense strength,' flashes on the solitaire's mind.

'The unknown is scary,' he thinks. 'In it I taste freedom. I feel the purity of the will to exist. Tears! There are tears flowing down my cheeks. I feel the mediocrity we have endured. I bear it. I cringe at our fall. It is our own doing. That is what hurts.'

'It is our weakness, the species' weakness that has caused us to be who we are. It can't be otherwise. We are accountable. Account for ourselves. Wrench ourselves free of the grips of dependency. *Demand* from ourselves and others!'

'I tremble, stagger at the ascent before us. "Onward," is the demand from within me. Blood rushes through me. The will to freedom surges from inside. With the force of my existence, existence itself I question the existence of the state.'

'Unlike science the state is not a form of paganism. It is a clumsy, overweight, stupid brute,' passes on his mind. 'It does not improve our lives rather it exploits our fear of the mortality illusion to get us to conform. The social contract does not exist, and instead the state threatens us with various reductions in the quality of our lives. If we are caught not conforming we are warned, fined, imprisoned, or even killed. It demands our obedience. It demands and coerces us to be weak. The state wants mediocrity and the more of it the better! It does not produce the strong. It produces the mediocre and feeds off them through money claims. It uses the mortality illusion to produce, control, and strengthen through them. In other words, the state uses weakness to produce and control weakness which increases its strength to produce and control more weakness.... The production and control of weakness is the basis of the state. It strengthens through the sweat and consciousness of the masses while all the time being dependent on the masses. It is not strength itself. It is strength contingent on the existence of weakness.'

'The state is a disaster. It has shielded us from the demand. We have become dependent on each other rather than ourselves. There is almost no accounted and account. There is exploitation of each other and nature. There is a No to existence! That is what the state demands from us. To be ourselves is to face the force of the state. To earn our existence is to lose what little freedom we have. We are relegated to the idleness of mediocrity.'

'To strengthen is to move. The state revolves around an increasing mass of weakness. It does not move or make us move. It does not produce the strong. Only existence can do that, and without the state.'

'Strength does not come from exploiting the mediocrity of the masses. Strength is something from inside. It comes from not exploiting weakness. It comes from us eliminating weakness and not being eliminated ourselves. Instead the state controls and feeds off us. "Take and appreciate what you get," it says while being convinced that we ought to be content and even grateful for its shield from the hard reality of existence.'

'The state is a thing of the past. It is from the dawn of the idea of life and death as truth. We have carried the idea a long, long way. For over two thousand years we have been weighed down by the certainty of death and the expectations of life. It is only now that we have the courage to call them non-truths. It is only now that the state's threats have lost their meaning. Fear of death, the basis for the state has been eliminated. It represents the inevitable end of the state as we know, and the resurgence of existence through all beings. And fear not! We will not wander in nothingness. We will exist with new meaning. Existence will be the state. We will be the state. There will be no exploitation. There will be earned elimination. We will not take for the sake of taking. We will take only what we need because to take more or less we become more a target of weakness, we become detached from ourselves. Instinct will guide us through and around the instinct of other beings. We must act. It is to earn our existence through our courage and honesty. It is to be on the path to the inevitable and endless *existence without weakness*.'

I am existence!

What Do Ice-picks Mean?

'I feel an even greater ascent,' the solitaire reflects. 'I feel myself soar to untold heights. There is a way out of our decadence. It is the *final* beast at the trough of mortality. It is to lower oneself into the depths of weakness.'

'I strike at the basis of the civilized world. I face the pastures of human decline. I am earthquake rumbling under almost all people. It is a moment of unprecedented change! I am defiant to the lies of the weak. I follow the voice from within that warns something is wrong. I am not fooled by the environment. The hatred of most the species does not deter me. I feel the dynamic of great change.'

'Though I hesitate. I stand to be despised and persecuted by those I care for. I feel the weight of the species bearing down on me. And yet freedom and truth is nearly my being! I don't seek to disparage. I seek to strengthen, to exist.'

'I feel the fire of existence inside and around. I feel myself becoming. I feel the strength. I know now. My words are for those who are worthy of them. My words, my blood are for those who have earned them. They are for the strong and nobody else.'

'I face the elusive marketplace. I face the supplier, provider of life and near death experiences. I face the thing to all people until now,' passes on his mind. 'I move beyond life and death, and therefore the

37

marketplace. I seek what nobody can supply and provide except for myself. I seek to earn existence for myself. There is nothing anybody else for can say or do. There is an exception. The strong can *reconfirm* what is already in me.'

'The marketplace has ceased to move. It cannot provide or supply what I demand. It has always been a place where the weak depend on each other. A place where the weak specialize to exploit each other. It is an expanding circle of weakness caused by taking more than we need and being almost unaccountable for it. Cowardliness and dishonesty is a perquisite for participating in it. There has to be an inner *denial* of who we are for us to participate in it. We have to convince ourselves that the marketplace is reality, and we do! It is not our fault, but it is our weakness. However, it will be our strength that will move us beyond it.'

'The marketplace is at its end. People are the force behind it, and we want to exist. It is an unconscious, restless force in us to preserve ourselves through earning our own existence. It cannot be stopped, and the marketplace *cannot* meet the demand. It tries by creating dangerous outdoor activities and selling us ice-picks and other accessories. It tries by escalating the violence and danger in spectator sports. The more it tries the more it stretches not only the limit of itself, but also the limit of the state's laws.'

'For the marketplace and state to stretch much further is to lose their meaning, to become absorbed into the vastness of existence. We are not waiting. The need to exist is so strong that we are putting ourselves into life threatening situations for the sake of them, and with or without the marketplace! In anything we excel at for the sake of excelling there is an element of strengthening through weakness, and even a suicidal urge to end our existence. The state does not let us act against weakness and the marketplace cannot supply the demand to exist so we turn on ourselves and each other. We are caught between the fabrications of the state and the realities of existence. We are confused. We know and feel there is more, but we don't know what it is. The control of morality, the distractions of science, the threats of the state, the seductions of the marketplace weigh down on our need to exist. We are trapped. And it is only our strength that can remove the weakness on us. We must not act for and from anybody else. We must act for and from ourselves. To do this we must *eliminate* the weakness on our own minds by cutting through fabrications with the question, 'what does it mean?''

'The end of civilization coincides with the end of the marketplace. It is to ascend from darkness to the light of existence. It is to move beyond the idea that we can produce greatness in things and through pursuits. It is to move beyond the idea that by meeting our material needs we will have an opportunity to attain and enjoy the highest states of being.'

'In the light we will not detach ourselves from existence to produce greatness. We will not focus on specific pursuits or things to produce greatness. We will become it ourselves! We will no longer produce things for others or do things for the sake of them. We will produce and act ourselves for ourselves. There will be no marketplace or civilization because there will be nothing to supply. There will be no need to produce great works of art or masterpieces. We will be them! We will concentrate solely on producing, existing the greatness of our beings. Our environment will be pure. We will earn the highest states of being. Our existence will be beyond the greatest art work imaginable. We will face the eternal accountability on our own.'

I am existence!

What Do Gravediggers Mean?

'Mortality, the great pessimism hangs over the species,' the solitaire reflects to himself. 'It is to be trapped by hopelessness. It is to be believe in limited movement. It is to cling to fading legacy.'

He looks around at the strong. "We have been fooled," he says to them. "We have overvalued ourselves and undervalued everything else. We do not have outlook. We focus on our lifetimes. It is hopeless because if death ends all meaning then everything before it ceases to have meaning. Our existence becomes decreasing degrees of nothingness."

One of the strong responds, "I don't understand. If there is no mortality what else could there be?"

"Mortality exists not as we perceive it. It exists as eternal *changing* states of being. We do not die. We are part of all other beings. There is

39

continual movement," replies the solitaire. "To move is to be clean. This is like our lifetimes. To *continually* move is to be pure. This is existence. Outside our minds there are no lifetimes. There are different forms of being in a continual movement to purity. We are flowing in and with existence from one form to another as we strengthen by existing who we are amongst all other beings doing likewise."

"Solitaire," says one of the strong, "we saw graveyards. We saw people being buried. We know we all end up in the ground. What else could there be?"

"The glorious, sagacious gravediggers thanks to Shakespeare and our gregariousness," he responds. "You saw into your *minds*. To see into existence is to go beyond the dead and burials. It is to see beings disposing of beings which pose a threat to our weakened existence. It is to see beings disposing of beings who are in transition to adding to the existence of other beings. It is to see beings covering up the process of our return to the vastness of existence."

"We return through the instinct or the force of existence of other beings. It passes through the reproductive cycle and into different forms. There is nothing created or destroyed. Everything moves along in one whole. Everything forms everything else."

"Existence is a timeless, endless whole. All beings are timeless and endless. There is no end or beginning to anything," says the solitaire. "The infinity of existence ensures that we never cease to exist. The eternal accountability ensures we never exist again as the same being."

"Nothing except existence itself has meaning," he says. "We are not dependent on all other beings rather they and ourselves form each other through constant universal interaction. There is no individual or collective of any kind. There is a limitless whole which we are moving parts of *without* our choice or doing. We exist endlessly in something without control over ourselves or anything. There are no stoppages. We are in continuous movement without any control of our own. It is as though we are floating endlessly through space."

"Yet there is meaning to our existence without us ourselves or the whole itself having meaning because existence is all there is. Hence, existence is the meaning of existence."

"Something just occurred to me," says one of the strong. "In existence without weakness what will happen to the past weakness if nothing is created or destroyed?"

"We are moving towards a state where all beings will earn their rightful existence according to their strength. There will be an equilibrium of strength made up all beings. The strong will form some beings whereas the weak will form other beings. There will be no weakness according to the forms of our being," says the solitaire. "We are *only* as free and pure as each other."

I am existence!

What Do Pits Mean?

In the glowing coals and ashes of the fire, the strong converse with each other. With his head tilting the solitaire listens.

"We have no control over anything," one of them blurts out. "What will happen will happen. There is nothing to earn or strive for. We don't earn our rightful existence we get it without any of our doing. And we have no choice. It is as if there is a master plan behind everything."

'I don't know when I will return or what form I will return as,' another thinks. 'I have no control so why does anything matter to me? Things will happen anyway.'

"Everything we do is not from ourselves," he remarks. "We are not trapped. We don't exist!"

"You are right. We don't exist because we are *never* the same. And there is nothing we can do about it because everything else determines what we do," responds one of them.

"We are just drifting endlessly. And even now as we talk," says another of the strong. "We can't think of ourselves or the whole because neither of them have meaning. There is the endless dynamic of strength through weakness, and we are part of it. There are no choices."

Nearby the weak watch with curiosity. "They're *all* mad," they whisper to each other.

The solitaire covers his face with his hands. 'We have fallen into nihilism,' flashes on his mind.

WHAT DO PITS MEAN?

"The only consolation is that we are never the same," another adds. "And it is not even our doing."

"What bothers me more than anything is that everything we do is condition on everything else," says one of them. "We are an endless whole and nothing else."

'There are no escapes from it,' the solitaire reflects to himself. 'We exist without our choice or doing, and there is *nothing* that can help us. We will know what we are meant to know.'

"The whole is in constant flux. We are in constant flux. The whole is never the same. We are never the same," the solitaire says to the strong. He picks up a handful of ashes and lets them fall.

"It's him," the weak whisper to each other.

"Our beings move from weakness to strength to elimination of weakness around endless other beings moving through the same cycle *though* at endless other stages," the solitaire continues. "There is a constant flux between those beings completing their cycles and new beings beginning their cycles. It is to be in the endlessness of strength through weakness on infinite levels. The continuous interaction of the cycles is the unfolding of existence. There is a constant strengthening and replenishing of beings. We use up our existence, and others replace us, and it does not stop. It is like there is wood always being placed in a fire and on wood that has almost had its time. It is like we are waves of an ocean followed by limitless other waves, and each wave representing a generation of people and amounting to no more than the ocean itself. And every ocean and wave, every tree and piece of wood is an assertion of existence. Everything by existing is an assertion of existence. Every assertion of existence is an assertion of the *will to exist*. It is the will to strengthen through weakness. It is the interaction of the will to strengthen through weakness by all things and beings which determines existence! And in all our own ways according to our form and force whether we are a wave or a human being we express no to mediocrity. We are part of the impulse of existence to strengthen and purify itself, and we act it out in our own way."

The strong move closer and listen.

"We are all part of the infinity of existence. We and others to follow, and ones that have past are part of the endless return of slightly different beings. We do not have to hope for a return. It is happening all the time," the solitaire says to them. "Every existing being is an example of eternal *changing* states of being. We have been mislead by the idea of self. There is no self because everything causes everything else. We are all inseparable parts of each other within a dynamic whole that is constantly unfolding. It is to be part of the constant interaction between changing strengths and weaknesses of being. There is no end to anything. There are no pits as we perceive them. A being does not just disappear. It merely changes form while remaining part of everything else. It is like a wave crashing onto a bank. Though the form of the wave ceases to exist, the wave itself returns to where it came from while another one replaces it! And it is these momentary forms, these assertions of existence with no more significance than anything else that we call selves! It is like we have gone on a walk and gave names and meaning to everything we saw based on our understanding of the individual things while not understanding how and why they interact as a whole. It is the *will to exist* behind the endless whole of existence, the endless state of everything causing everything that has and will *only* have meaning."

I am existence!

What Do Mourners Mean?

"What do we do? Where do we go?" one of the strong asks.

The solitaire lowers his head. He cannot respond what he knows; and yet he feels an impulse to tell everything he knows, to open his heart, to ask for guidance, to have somebody tell him where he has gone wrong. Similar to the highest flame above, he turns and walks away.

'I am alone,' he cries from within.

The strong stand motionless. There are tears in some of their eyes. "Solitaire we are with you," one of them says to himself. Others move towards him and then stop.

'Where will I go? What will I do?' flashes on his mind. 'I am an endless slave to existence. We all are. Is that what they want to hear? There is no hope! There is no escape even for those who think they can control their own existence by controlling others. To attempt this is like trying to control the motion of the planet or the amount of light radiated by the sun. It will either be futile or a disaster. We cannot escape that we are in a timeless, endless whole where everything causes everything else. With everything never the same and caused by everything else we can't even influence others!'

The weak stare and curse at him as he wanders by.

'Are we going to feel sorry for ourselves for our reality?' he asks himself. 'Are we going to mourn the loss of all meaning to our existence? It is only the weak that feel pity and sorrow for themselves and others. It is only the weak that believe in the self and conform to it. Purity is the call from within me. There is no hope, but I cling to the will to strengthen through weakness. There is no hope, but I strengthen by moving with the whole. Though I drift endlessly I have to do something. I cling to the purity of the dynamic. I will strive every waking moment to eliminate the weakness of our existence!'

He rests behind several coals on ashes.

'To move with the dynamic is to move with meaning itself,' he says to himself. 'It is to become the closest thing to truth and honesty. It is to become a *force* of existence. I surrender to the dynamic. I become it. I flow endlessly with meaning. I radiate out like the sun and effect all beings. There is our destiny. It is to transcend the norms of mediocrity. It is to be guided by not the illusion of death, but the force of existence. It is to free oneself from the fabrications on our minds, and be the power of existence from within.'

'We can control and influence! To do this we must cut ourselves off from the rest. Only in our own space can we know and be who we are, and thereby influence almost all beings. To do otherwise is to be controlled and influenced by everybody else,' the solitaire reflects.

He rises from the ashes and stretches out his arms. 'I have *found* a way,' flashes on his mind. 'And it is only for those who truly earn it. We can never escape reality though we can determine how it influences who we are. It is to act from within rather than without.'

'I have returned to where I was though I am strengthened with wisdom. I return to independence of being as the only way. I return to its power! It is to transcend the endless whole and master over it. It is to endure solitude and overcome ourselves, and therefore everybody else. It

44

is to act and breath from the will to power! It is to be the force of existence from within and without. We are movers of the whole while never being in it. We act from existence and nothing else. It is to ascend to the highest state of being. It is to go beyond the *threshold* of existence. It is be the supreme controller of everything, even existence itself.'

The solitaire makes a fist in triumph of the will of existence.

He releases it as he returns to his thoughts. 'The blade of honesty; the courage to *strike*,' he thinks to himself.

'The self has always been in the way. It is like a dam utilizing and regulating our existence. It is like numbers on our backs as a way to identify who we are. Instead we are given names. We do not think. We see a being and assume it is a single being, a self. There is no thought about almost everything causing everything else. It is to perceive in the most narrow outlook, and almost the whole world is based on it! In the spirit of Aristotle we classify and codify everything we sense *without* knowing how everything interacts. It is like we have created pieces of an imaginary puzzle out of all the things we sense, and we spend the rest of our time trying to force them together. For us to say that we are all an endless whole is to make people think and fear that we are taking something from them. And we are! We are taking off the rusty shackles of self that people have been dragging for over two thousand years, and in return giving them freedom.'

'The idea of self has been and will always be a way to make us accountable not to ourselves, but to those who are behind the legislation and enforcement of law. The self divides and fragments us. We become selves or accountable ends though in existence there is no such thing as an end. We become good and bad selves to give meaning to the law of others over us. We are taught that the self equates with freedom and independence without really knowing why. We attach to ourselves while at the same time attaching to metal bars that separate us from each other! We do not flow with each other and existence. We clink along from the shackles of our illusory selves. It is to be caged by our fabricated personalities, expectations, responsibilities and the law of self, and with the only exit being death. We have created an existence of suffering and fear which has no correlation to existence itself. To have an individual

45

self defies any sense of existence because it means to exist beyond existence. Not even a being who has earned the will to power can be called an individual self! He is a pure force of existence and nothing more. And yet the individual self is the basis of our existence. We have not surpassed existence. We have chained our wills by our perception of who we are. It is a constraint, and oh it is limiting! It prevents us from existing who we are.'

'To overcome the self is eliminate the basis for law. It is to eliminate the illusions of marriage, property, taxation, morality, life, and death. To eliminate law is to eliminate the basis for civilization. It is to open the way for a new will to power! It is to flow according to the universal pulse of strength through weakness.'

'We will move and thereby strengthen because we have to. We will know each other according to the power of our wills and brains. Our language will be the universal language of existence, the language of strength through weakness. Increasing simplicity through earned strength will define who and what we are. It defines the new will to power.'

I am existence!

What Do Tombstones Mean?

'There are changing states of being. If only we could exist them,' the solitaire thinks to himself. 'Solitude is the sacred gateway, the sacred journey to them. It is to return to ourselves and overcome them. Though there are *few* that have the courage and honesty. And even many of those who do enter fail to reach the opening to existence. They don't overcome their selves. Their selves overcome them! And that is how it should be. The will to power is only for truly great beings. It is to pass through the most extreme tests of existence. It is to pull out of the distractions, temptations, exploitations of the world and face the weakness of the species on our own, and eliminate it. It is to come out of solitude existing solely from within, and therefore from *everywhere*.'

'I demand stronger people, a stronger species!' the solitaire erupts from within. 'The time has come to move. The tidal wave of independence of being has appeared. It is a wave of change, a movement of the whole. It cannot be stopped. The shackles of self have been broken through and swept away. There is no death or morality. The laws of self have become meaningless. A new being, a new species has arisen from our weakness. A being, a species that is fearless and willing to sacrifice itself for the meaning of strength through weakness. It is to demand a new standard. Those who resist the wave of independence of being will be crushed by its force. Those who do not will ride it to higher states of being. It will become them, and they will become it.'

The solitaire lowers himself onto ashes.

'I have been fooled by myself. I am not ready. I am still in the darkness of solitude! To attach to myself is to attach to disaster. I am lost in my thoughts. To proceed is to continue without guidance or direction. It is to enter the infinite unknown and drift in nothingness.'

'Where did I go wrong?' he asks himself. 'It is the self. I can't get away from it. It has blocked my ascent. To go ahead is to be crushed under it. To remain where I am is to linger in darkness. I am afraid to move ahead. I feel the power, and yet I can't make the first step through myself. I don't know how to proceed. I sense the form of the great being, but I can't process it into thoughts.'

'I want to know what it means to perceive eternal *changing* states of being,' passes on his mind. 'What are the thoughts of such a being? To know them is to become the new will to power.'

'To perceive the constant movement and change of all beings is to be a great being. It is to exist without attachments,' reflects the solitaire. 'It is to perceive eternal *changing* states of being in all things. To do this a great being must exist strength through weakness in his every thought and action. There are no compromises ever. There is clarity and purity of earned strength. The great being must always act as existence demands. He must know that what passes will never return, and how things pass is what he can control. The great being must seize each and ever moment with the will to power! It is to control the fleeting present of beings, and therefore the past and future of them. What distinguishes the great being from others must be the strength of his courage to stay true to what he knows and we all know while existing amidst weakness. And it is only through the weakness of others that he can earn the power of existence just as it is only through the strength of others that he will return to who he really is or never transcend it.'

'The will to power is a temporary phenomena because it is merely a means of existence to respond to an increase in weakness. We are all ebbing and flowing, strengthening and weakening in the endless whole. There is no escape not even through the will to power. Our purpose is to exist and nothing else. The great being is not sought. It is not a heightened state of being which everybody should aspire for. Existence uses that rare being to eliminate excessive weakness. And it is only the same weakness that makes *great* beings like Napoleon and Nietzsche what they are! Though they are no less part of everything than anybody else.'

'There is no escape for any of us, and not even under tombstones or as great beings,' the solitaire says to himself. 'I have gone to the end of existence, and I was at it all the time. I am lost in everything I know and confused by everything I don't know.'

He motions his arms to feel for almost anything.

Sensing the glow of a coal, he wanders towards and past it with his hand pressed against his forehead.

'I have nothing to say to the strong except that things are as they should be,' passes on his mind. 'It is our strength *and* weakness that has lead us to where we are, and it will be them that will lead us into the future. Is there a better way than some people gaining at the expense of others? Why should some people be better off than others in existence where everything causes everything else? Since we are parts of existence and always will be, it doesn't make sense why we don't make it the basis for how we exist.'

'From everything I have learned it is independence of being that stands out. There is nothing that can surpass us earning our existence for ourselves. Everything we do should reflect the whole of existence because we are nothing more or less than the whole. To make the whole strong and pure requires that we become strong and pure. To make us pure and strong we require independence of being. There is no other way to truly strengthen ourselves than to do it ourselves around every other being doing likewise.'

'We have an opportunity through independence of being to eliminate our disgust at ourselves and existence. It is a tragedy for people to not value their fleeting existence when it could be otherwise. It is a tragedy for the species to become weaker through its own weakness. The universal pulse of existence is strength through weakness, and that should be no different for us.'

He looks down at ashes and then above at the brightness of the flames.

'There is no should,' he says to himself. 'We are all part of an endless whole in which everything is what it is and nothing else. It is only a new will to power that can redirect ourselves and the species. Anything else is merely part of the flow of previous assertions of mediocrity.'

I am existence!

What Do Blades Of Grass Mean?

'The pain, the sacrifice to go forward to merely tread on new ground. It's hard, so hard,' the solitaire says to himself. 'I have lost blood, and yet there is still further to go. I am alone facing a steep, icy ascent which could give us meaning to our existence, which could take us out of the darkness of mediocrity and into the lightness of strength. I have climbed so high that to turn back would be a disaster while to go forward risks disaster. Every move has become either fatal or a struggle.'

'And I *know* the basic forces of our existence,' he says to himself from high up in the ranges of existence. 'There is the core of the masses or the will to exist beside assertions of mediocrity, and it is the will to power which offsets mediocrity, and thereby frees the masses' natural tendency to exist. However, it is weakness in the masses which causes assertions of mediocrity, and weakness in the mediocrity which causes the will to power, and then weakness in the will to power which causes the will to exist. We exist in a rotating triangular relationship of offsetting sides within fluctuating strengths and weaknesses. It is to move around and around while gradually contracting inward to the essence of our beings.'

WHAT DO BLADES OF GRASS MEAN?

The solitaire takes a breath. He looks up at light shimmering off the peaks.

'The masses are like logs on a fire, the assertions of mediocrity the flames feeding off the them, and the will to power an occasional gust which challenges the flames. It all makes sense. And yet where does our weakness come from? To answer that is to know everything there is to know. Again I return to the eternal dynamic of strength through weakness. Weakness is the basis for everything and including existence itself. And it is strength that moves us gradually to greater strength and purity. Our only purpose is to exist through the elimination of weakness.'

'The eternal accountability makes the assertions of mediocrity redundant. The fire of existence is all around. Our weakness comes from ourselves. We have succumbed to the assertions of mediocrity which have dragged us into the depths of meaninglessness. We are being gradually bleed by them because they are expansive, and they exist solely off our weakness. And it will only be our strength that will free us from them. It is to overcome the asserters of mediocrity with a new will to power from the masses of the species. It is to act with long awaited meaning by acting against the asserters, the real weakness of the species. It is to topple them through a vast surge of the new will to power, and thereby end our suffering from the constant and painful linear rotation of our existence.'

'Enough!' is the thunder from the peaks of existence. 'I am an avalanche of avalanches heading with deadly force towards the asserters of mediocrity. It is an unstoppable force of strength against and through the weakness that has been feeding, for too long, off the species! It is to ascend the strong, the worthy into a higher state of being. A state where we do the best we can in the reality of everything causing everything else in an infinite whole. A state where our only meaning comes from moving to greater strength and freedom. It is to end the boredom, the meaninglessness of others doing what we can do ourselves! It is to breath the exultation of earning our existence for ourselves. It is to become with meaning, the only meaning of who we are: the will to exist. Through the power of our force making contact, we earn our ascent beyond the asserters of mediocrity, the states, the religions, the sciences,

50

the marketplaces, and into existence: an environment from which stronger and purer beings *and* species will rise out of.'

The solitaire looks out from the summit of existence. The sky is clear with the warm rays of the sun passing through it. More than twenty-five hundred feet below him the avalanche had done its work.

'It is time to come together brothers and sisters of existence. We are no longer alone drifting in nothingness,' he says. 'We are part of existence and united with blades of grass and almost all other beings through our wills to exist in the infinite whole. It is to be from existence and nothing else. It is to act together in the dynamic uniformity of existence without any orders except from within. There are no taxes, faiths, or pledges of allegiance nor are there anthems or flag waving. We do not have nationalities or ethnicities. We are free to exist with the only demand being that we earn our existence. And we do by acting out our instincts of strength through weakness. It is to eliminate, within our means, mediocrity. It is to ascend beyond the controls of the law of self and exist as *one* with the universal, impartial demand of the eternal accountability.'

'Existence is where we have always been from. Though it is only now after overcoming our own weakness that we can take unoffending pride in who and what we are. We have *eliminated* the self, the cause of our loneliness and fears, and found harmony between our instincts and existence. We have earned the feeling of trust and knowing of belief in the power and purity of existence which has *always* been lacking in other things. We have taken ourselves out of our empty, dull existence which seems to pass by with almost no purpose, and earned the force of meaning which can only come from existence itself. It is to overcome the illusory void in us, and thus set our beings free for us to exist as we are meant to be.'

He feels a breeze against his face as his view passes over the vast mountainous surroundings.

'We are part of everything and always will be,' he thinks to himself.

He takes a step upward onto the highest peak of existence and breaths the pure air, the earned freedom, the *oneness* with existence.

'We are warriors of existence, and therefore *everything*,' a voice echoes.

I am existence!

PART TWO: WITHIN THE SURRENDER

FREEDOM FANTASY

What Do Candy Bars Mean?

Downward on the other side of the highest peak of existence, the solitaire rests in a cave.

'I can't go any further,' he says to himself. He lowers his head against folded arms. 'I am alone,' passes on his mind as a tear surfaces to his eyes.

'It is the work of the self which wants to exist like almost anything else.'

Outside the cave and in darkness the sound of a wolf howling echoes.

'We are warriors of existence. We are warriors of existence. We are warriors of existence,' the solitaire says. 'It can't be denied or stopped. To exist is to exist, no matter what we are, by strength through weakness. How heroic we are and nothing else is what distinguishes us from each other.'

He clutches his head and says, 'I've been wrong, so wrong. We have all been wrong. We attach to the idea of freedom as though it is the most desirable existence, and yet it is nothing more than a distraction from who we are. It is like the sweet taste of a candy bar, and ends up doing more harm to us than good. We don't earn freedom for ourselves. It comes packaged like candy with the only requirements that some of us vote and most of us pay for it with our sweat and blood. The state provides and gives us it through maintaining and expanding infrastructure, and creating and enforcing laws centered around us both using it and interacting with each other. And somehow magically from this controlled and crowded environment we have the means to freedom. It is like a dinner which others prepare for us, wait on us, and clean up after us, and the only requirements are that some of us show up and most of us *pay* the bill at the end. And almost all of us during and after the dinner call it freedom.'

'The idea of freedom is a drug of the mind administered by the state and its associates to control us by making it seem that we are existing in an environment which is the most conducive to satisfying our manufactured desire for freedom. It is like a pill that makes us at ease with our environment while never satisfying our desire for freedom itself, and thus causing us to expend ourselves in the attempt. We never attain that elusive freedom because there is no freedom to attain. Instead we are on treadmill which only benefits those who are not on it by asking us to pay up for using it. We are like a donkey chasing a carrot though in our case we are chasing the illusion of freedom.'

'Freedom is nothing more than a symbol or word that describes a state of being with minimal constraints. There has never been and nor will there ever be freedom itself. The best way to describe the meaning of freedom in the world is freedom of self or in other words the iron ball fastened to the shackles around our ankles. The iron ball is simply an illusion of existence and reality of our minds *contingent* on the shackles of self. It does not give us liberated movement rather it keeps us constrained by the burden of ourselves.'

'Every freedom we exist and even risk our lives for such as freedom to vote, freedom of speech, and freedom of press are merely extensions of the self; and we already know that the self is an entrapment because it has no correlation to existence where everything causes everything else in an endless flow.'

'The state and of course through our own doing has denied us existence from our instincts, and instead it controls us through our manufactured consciousness which keeps who we are locked away in solitary cells never to be opened unless the state lets us or we open them ourselves. To open them ourselves we must overcome the illusions of self, and therefore the state and civilization. To not do this is to continue to exist as half-beings at best while being controlled by the leash and stick of the state, and its sweet biscuits of freedom.'

'Through the illusion of freedom the state has herded and entrapped us in a concrete pen in which we are forced to obey the laws of the pen or face the inevitable consequences. Our snorts or cries of freedom in the pen is nothing more than the cry of the herd. We have been so mislead by the state and ourselves that we don't even know why we attach to freedom or what it means, and yet it is the guiding force of our all too short existence. We exist in the manufactured fantasies of our minds without noticing the ball and chain, but in hard reality we are alienated from most people and reasonably obedient to the demands of the state. We are afraid to earn our existence for ourselves, and instead we look for an easy way out which amounts to giving up who we are for the deceptive freedom of self. It is to become mere pawns of the state who in the end will always look after itself. And even if we are convinced that we earn material freedom what do we do with it and where do we go with selves that can never be satisfied? There is nothing we can do except try and satisfy our always changing wants and desires while the secret to a meaningful existence lies locked away inside us. It amounts to a painful, fleeting existence in which we are deprived of existing who we are while being driven to produce for the benefit of others through a vain, lifelong struggle to meet superficial standards and illusory expectations all in an attempt to satisfy our unsatisfiable selves.'

'Freedom and its counterpart slavery are part of a list of dichotomies such as life and death, good and bad, reward and punishment, pleasure and pain, and gain and loss which the state uses to divide, and therefore control us, and *also* to justify its environment and demands. It is a form of systematic control designed for the preservation of the state and its associates. The single lever of control is comparisons of people and states. Through mass media the state continual draws on the dichotomies embedded in our minds for its own advantage whether criticizing another state for its failure to recognize human rights, or praising individuals for their obedience to the marketplace, and therefore to the state.'

'We exist in a mass confusion of values and ideas which only those on the outside have control while rest of us are cast adrift in tides created by them. Our minds are like game machines in which those playing them merely have to keep the ball or words in play and hit the scores or latent values on our minds. It is like the word democracy which the state uses to conjure the fantasy of freedom and the illusion of order and fairness, and thus direct and guide the masses for its own benefit, or the flaunt of the wealthy which money-makers use to create an illusion of happiness and well-being for a similar purpose. And this is the reality of the world and freedom where everything revolves around the few getting the masses to produce from their sweat and blood for the few's own benefit.

The only defense is to scrutinize, from who we are, our thoughts and values.'

I am existence!

What Do Buck Teeth Mean?

'I don't feel alone,' the solitaire says to himself. 'I am surpassing myself and connecting with everything else.' He sits hunched against a wall with his arms folded on his knees.

The near darkness outside adds a glimmer of light to the cave.

'The power of solitude,' flashes on his mind. 'It is to be lost in the ideas of others and our own while gradually finding, through sheer struggle, our way to who we are. Every step away from ourselves is a step closer to the power of existence. Our purpose is to exist from our beings which can only happen through our detachment from the self. Any feelings of depression or loneliness is the work of it through the manufactured herd instinct, and to break through the self is to become *consciously* part of existence.'

'And when the self is bleeding us with false hopes and expectations, and mediocre standards we ask the question, what does it mean? and keep answering it until we root-out the weakness. We cannot go wrong because the self has to show its masked face to do its work and the question if used with courage and honesty will always get beneath its insidious surface.'

'Freedom of self means the freedom of the self and indirectly the state to control who we are. The state gives meaning to the self because its laws are based on it through categorical non-freedoms which means impermissible freedoms that are either to the state's disadvantage or threats to it while at the same time allowing all other freedoms which are either to the state's advantage or are not practical for it to legislate. In other words, we are caught between the state trying to contain who we are through laws of self while allowing out of necessity for us to exist as we are. It is to be in constant conflict between our being and an impersonator over the same thing, and with the state watching and ready to pounce on us from a distance.'

FREEDOM FANTASY

'Religion and science have taken advantage of the state's far from perfect environment by offering their *own* freedoms to the masses. And as we know freedom is just a means to control others through their credulousness of what the word means and ignorance of what it really means. To avoid conflict with the state and its laws by going beyond its permissible freedoms, these other asserters deny and postpone our illusory freedom through manufactured self-denial of the state's freedoms. Expressed another way, they relieve our constant confusion and struggle over who we are by offering ways out of our existence and at the same time misleading us with their own notions of freedom. It is to take advantage of the state's unappetizing freedom or candy bar by offering one with a different flavour or postponing one altogether for an imaginary super bar. These asserters are not stupid because to have a claim, regardless of its truth, on the means to freedom is to have potential control over the masses. And yet for anybody to give up what freedom the state allows for even less freedom is to be defeated by their *self*. It is to surrender to an almost exclusive sanctuary of the self while suppressing our being. These people or *ascetic-selves*, and there are many of them, are an abnormal outgrowth out of the state's controlled environment similar to buck teeth because they cannot handle the pressure around them. They have succumbed to weakness instead of standing their ground or taking the mask off the self with the question, what does it mean?'

'The religious are not fools though they have contempt for us, and that is their weakness. We are not all stupid enough to believe that there is super bar called immortal freedom from another word called God, and yet the religious are cunning enough to take advantage of the state's failings. They stand on street corners handing out leaflets and muttering a way out to people caught in a whirlwind of confusion and struggle between the self and our being while trying to stay clear of the fistful whims of the state. They do not ask people to be strong from within rather they ask them to give up, and people do in their own way by the thousands. It is to enter the sanctuary of the self and misperceive it for the sanctuary of the litany of words or names like Saviour, Lord, Shepherd, Christ, Father, True one, Chosen One, Great One, God, Almighty which all have same meaning: *nothingness* and while all the time the self feasts on our weakness. Fool yourself not! It is the self and nothing else that has been and will always be hiding behind these all too real escapes into our imagination. The religious merely show the way by reminding us of the ever so sweet super bar. It is to transcend the analogy of the donkey chasing the carrot to a person chasing the ideas of others on his mind or a person sitting in a Ferris wheel going around and around while being convinced he is somewhere else. And at least the donkey can see the carrot.'

'Realizing that it would impossible to do anything beyond what the religious offer, the corporate sciences focus solely on the present and carve out niches of freedoms to attract the masses, and then exploit them. It is a risky approach because the masses can see the surface of what they offer just like the donkey can see the carrot, and therefore unlike the donkey they could see beyond it. However, the corporate sciences have nothing to lose because the state and religious have made a mess of what they offer, and nobody as of now has actually exposed the self and freedom of self for what they are. And the sciences know our game machines and the high points scored by hitting and keep hitting the 'new' and glitz values, and the mega points scored by hitting the gold bell of the self. Also, they know the state and its needs to maintain its control and to get people to produce. These are the *pragmatists* who capitalize on the situation or environment as it is. They have by getting millions upon millions of people to sit in front of computer and television screens instead of existing for themselves and while keeping the state more than content with part of their catch.'

'All the ascetic-selves do in front of these screens is let others control their existence while they convince themselves that they have somehow avoided what the state and religious offer. Ironically, they have entered another sanctuary of the self where instead of saying and chanting prayers or existing as the state demands they are satiated with knowledge and information that has almost no practical use. That is the whole point. To deny and even escape from the reality of state's environment and what the religious offer by existing what another power offers and convincing themselves that it is the way out for them though they are really a part of the masses which does not have enough strength to see the beyond the manipulation of the corporate sciences, and thereby exist for themselves and even question the sciences all too obvious weakness.'

The solitaire moves further into the cave for more warmth and solitude.

'The criteria to determine our freedom is not whether we have exercised freedom of choice or action as the state and other asserters want us to believe rather it is whether we are existing from who we are,' he says to himself.

'We, the strong are not mislead by the self or anything else into thinking we need to escape or find a way out of the state's environment. We find a way to strengthen *through* it, and therefore through the self itself.'

I am existence!

What Do Cavities Mean?

'The law of self is a disaster which has made our existence a constant conflict between the self and who we are,' the solitaire thinks. 'It is how the state to divides us ourselves in two, and therefore has control over us. We are to blame for accepting all the sweet candy bars the state professes to offer us, and thus denying ourselves the strength of *using* our teeth or earning our *own* existence for ourselves. Instead our existence is almost meaningless, and our teeth have cavities from sucking on the sweets of what others have done and continue to do for us. That is the state's idea of freedom in which everybody ought to ease their way through existence because the state's looking after us whether we like it or not. We are like children at recess with teachers standing by to make sure they are well-behaved and within a fenced off area partly separating them from the reality of existence or like people hospitalized receiving all their needs from without except that we have more space to move around in and are a few steps closer to doing things ourselves.'

'It is hard, but we *must* face the weakness to move beyond it,' he says to himself.

'The state has almost eliminated our inherent freedoms with the demands that we don't harm anybody else and we pay taxes which

61

translate into a demand on us to produce to pay taxes and reproduce to keep paying them. As we know already that the state looks after its own interests. The key word it uses to deny us our freedom and thereby control who we are is the word *harm*. It does this by making almost all physical harm except for self-defense illegal and enforces it through intimidation, fines, and imprisonment. Yet, the state leaves a hole in the law pertaining to mental harm *for* it and others to play our games machines. The hole in mental harm is representation or more accurately *misrepresentation* of things which the state surrounds with laws against slander, threats, forms of harassment, and even misrepresentation on such things as food items because that interferes with our reproduction. However, almost anything else is open for any of us to misrepresent to our advantage which about sums up the marketplace. And it is the state that not only allows us to be dishonest to each other, but encourages us, for its own benefit, to be dishonest to each other while covering up this inconsistency with the misleading claim that freedom of speech and press must be upheld.'

'Through the gradual systematization of law the state has channeled the power of who we are into the endless domain of our consciousness while controlling everything outside it. Our consciousness is the lone battlefield in which we can act out ourselves by deceiving and cheating each other, and be rewarded for it through each others earnings. We should not be surprised because the state has merely created what it considers the best environment for its preservation.'

'Just as the law of self has been narrowed down to our consciousness our freedoms have been narrowed down to the lone and yet truly powerful freedom we have, the freedom to think. It is to give us recourse to the infinite domain of our thoughts which nobody, but ourselves have direct control over. And if there was a choice to what single freedom we could have anybody with any sense would choose the freedom to think because to lose it is to lose control over who we are whereas to have it is to control our conscious existence. Nevertheless, those that make use of this freedom by thinking for themselves are rare.'

'Although it requires concentrated effort to think with meaning, it doesn't make sense why more of us do not think for ourselves. To do so is to act from who we are and strengthen through the weakness on

62

our minds, and thus influence the causes for our continued preservation while to not do so is to let the ideas of others fill our minds and influence not the causes for our preservation, but their own. And to think itself is not enough. We must think as a means to move and act from instinct which will only happen if we ourselves clean our minds by making our values and beliefs accountable.'

'The state is vulnerable because it can never control how we think. Hence, it always exists with internal vulnerability which it tries to *contain* by attempting to control what we think. To do this it attempts to control our environment while maintaining a semblance of so-called freedom. It is trapped because to rule by the idea of freedom goes against its instinct to preserve itself while the idea of freedom is the basis for its right to rule. To cope with this inherent conflict it reduces our freedom from who we are while increasing the freedom of the self which it has more control over. Also, it increases its control over our environment. The next step is to have more and more control over our movement inside and outside the state, or in other words to eventually contain us in an environment which it controls. This is the ideal situation for any power seeking control over others because to control a person's environment, from the first moment of his existence, is to control what he thinks. The state already partly does this through the marketplace which compensates for the difficulty of controlling our movement, and thereby allows the state to focus its effort on restricting the ideas assessable to us by indoctrinating us with values and beliefs through the educational system, marketplace itself, and symbols like flags, anthems, and role models.'

'The state has trapped itself because it can only impose its calculated values and beliefs from the outside while we have and will always have control over whether they have any meaning.'

'We face a hard task because to be honest in the marketplace is to offer what almost nobody wants and to exist in the state's environment is to face the symbols and values from the state and other asserters. There is an opening if we can see through the marketplace and indoctrination. It is to direct our thoughts through the hole in the law of self by using our minds not to misrepresent things, but to represent things as they are. More than that we can reach others with the truth by criticizing old ideas and sharing new ones. The revolution begins on our minds. We have the freedom to think, and therefore to make it happen by entering the battlefield of our consciousness as warriors of existence. We have the opportunity to strike and slash through the weakness that has been gradually bleeding the species of its existence, and to eventually climb beyond steep slopes to the peaks of existence with ideas and values which will enliven us with the will to exist. This is not a courageous journey to be who we are. It is a journey to ensure our survival by becoming and earning who we are. There is nothing that can stop us except the self which we must overcome if we are to reach new heights and meaning. The only way to do this is to strike with solitude, honesty, and courage. As one force they are like an acid that burns through to what is truly strong or even more, like a great being's mind that cuts from the power of instinct to the essence of any idea and rejects it or adds it to its system of thought. To earn this threesome force is to break through the most stringent social conditioning by the state: the idea that we are social beings.'

'The state, the other asserters, and the masses of weak that follow them will do everything in their power short of denying us freedom of thought to stop us from deconstructing civilization. We must not mistake that we are a threat to their way of existence, and will be treated as enemies which could result in an expansion of the battlefield from our minds to outside them *and* at minimum repeated attempts by the state to indoctrinate the masses with lies about us. However, the blaze of truth on our minds can only be extinguished by greater truths which would only add to our will to exist and will to return the species to the purity of existence. To deny us freedom of speech and press through censorship and cries of sedition is merely to delay the spread of the fire on our minds and its inevitable regrowth from the pure seed of existence. To imprison and murder some of us, and thereby break their own laws to deny some of us freedom of thought is to strengthen our will to exist by exposing what the state and the other asserters really are. It is to get the state, and therefore the others as well, to tear off its own mask and uncover the monster! and other monsters for all to see. We are an invincible force because it is existence and nothing else which we are coming from, and it is the fatal weakness of the state and the other asserters, the irreparable hole in the law of self which we are charging and strengthening through.'

I am existence!

What Do False-teeth Mean?

Memories of his struggle *after* struggle in the world flash on the solitaire's mind.

'I will be strong,' he says to himself, 'and fight through the lasting attempts by the weak to distract me and even lower me into their mediocrity. And it's not them; it's the work of the self through them and ultimately *myself* which is trying to preserve itself.'

'I cannot forget,' he says with his hands pressing against his face, 'that the question, what does it mean? what does it mean? what does it mean? is my and our means of survival. It is to enter the battlefield of our minds armed with swords from who we are, and to do otherwise is to be rendered defenseless against the cunningness and maliciousness of the self who has almost limitless disguises and methods though it will always be constrained by the amount of weakness on our minds. To clean our minds is to eliminate the basis for the rank weeds of the self; and we know that any outer display of extreme emotion whether happiness or sadness, love or hatred, and depression or joy is a sign of the self because its objective is to stray us from the purity of who we are, and thereby thrive in weakness. It is in these moments when the self tries to spread itself to others or reinforce its hold on us while facing the possibility of exposing itself to our instinct, and what it fears most is the question, what does it mean? We must apply it with the tenacity and dexterity of a gardener using a spade to remove a weed and its roots. To not apply it is to face the ever present danger of personalizing our difficulties or getting distracted by the self's disguise which may be coming at us in numerous forms one after the other and repeated over again and again in slightly different forms. It is to be like a green gardener who goes after the leaves and stems of weeds with his bare hands while leaving behind their roots and tiring himself, and with himself only to have to repeat and keep repeating it until he either realizes a more effective way or gives up. In such a situation we must pull back and apply the question to our own emotions and perceptions because it is only from a stable base that we can deal with the onslaught of weakness directed at us by the self from around.'

'To get us to personalize is the malicious work of the self, and to eliminate this tendency is to pull the weed of all weeds of the self out by its roots. It is a formidable, but not impossible task which requires a prolonged effort on our part using the threesome force. And every movement away from the self is a movement towards the serenity and power of who we are. The hardest step is the first because it is to make the immutable break with the self or declaration of war on it from the battlefield of our minds, around the infantry of our intellect, and beside the heavy cannon of our instinct.'

'For us the war has long been commenced, and right now we face with our cannon the categorical freedom called slavery which some asserters use to justify their own means by creating the antithesis, freedom and slavery, and thus a misleading comparison between themselves and the state. The cry from amongst us is not that of freedom, but the unanimous thunder from inside us, 'Existence! Hurrah!' And the blasts from the cannon ruptures the idea of slavery and exposes the truth that there is *no* such thing as total control by one person over another. Rather there are endless changing states of control of one person over another. Without even a counter strike, the white flag of slavery is raised by the self in disguise of these asserters and in vain because we know it is just another disguise of the self, the worn cloak of morality. So the cannon fires another volley while the infantry charge in with the insight that slavery is merely a word which corresponds to an illusion of our minds where slavery is a state of less freedom than others. However, in existence we know slavery is nothingness because everything causes everything else, and therefore if slavery really existed everything must be slavery which is absurd because it is impossible to be enslaved to who we are. There is only a master, or endless whole, and no slave.'

From a hilltop the solitaire stands and looks yonder over the battlefield, and then turns away with disgust.

'We have been mislead,' flashes on his mind. 'We went after the obvious when we should have known that the self is far more deceptive than that. It has chosen the most elusive worldly creation to hide behind: the marketplace.'

'Slavery is a distraction and the marketplace at the same time,' he reflects. 'We are caught by the contrast between the outside and inside of our minds though they are part of the same thing which amounts to a form of slavery. The marketplace does not have direct, physical control over us rather it has physical control over us through our minds. And it is the state and other asserters behind the marketplace, and the self behind them while our minds are full of planted images, ideas, values, and beliefs from the state's environment and with the silver ball called our thoughts hitting and spinning almost continuously off them and causing us to act as we do except for increasingly rare moments when our instinct *actually* guides our actions. In order to get a conception of how controlled we are, and to do this we must overcome the self which is preventing us from sharpening our perspective. We have to look at the whole picture that our minds like tiny games machines in almost continuous play and contingent on the giant games machine called the marketplace. Yet almost everything we think and do is against this because it is not us acting or thinking rather we are dependent on others doing and thinking things for us. It is to lose control over our own preservation while not even being aware of it because it stems from our minds which we believe to be from who we are. Our minds are like having false-teeth and not asking ourselves what they mean, and thus miss an opportunity to penetrate to the self's control over us not just through our fake teeth and fake minds, but to the causes that lead to our physical and mental decline, and dependency on others. The result is that we lose our teeth in vain and enter our own minds as strangers.'

'The system through misrepresentation or the hole in the law of self is contingent on stability in the numbers of those that misrepresent and those that are deceived by it. A decrease in those that are deceived or an increase in those that misrepresent while not increasing the things that are misrepresented will put more pressure on those who misrepresent to intensify it with the looming danger of exposing themselves for what they are. As it stands the few misrepresent with a mixture of non-truth and truth. However, as we strengthen through our freedom to think, and therefore through the weakness on our minds, the few will have to misrepresent with more non-truth and less truth. This is a natural growth first stemming from our weakness and their strength, and now our strength and their weakness, and leading to a state where there are many who misrepresent and few who are deceived and beyond this where there are only those that exist. It is to evolve past the dichotomies of misrepresent and represent, and non-truth and truth, and into a state of not indirect or direct physical control over each other, but everything flowing together in the endless whole according to the eternal dynamic. To move the other way towards more representation is to move to the same end in which people *will not* want to produce for others because it requires too much effort or is impossible. And instead they will produce for *themselves* and even if it's through others. In either scenario, there is a gradual movement by us to greater accountability and strength which cannot be stopped. What the state and other asserters are working towards is creating an environment in which we completely surrender to the self, thus to their control which will never happen as long as we have and exercise the freedom to think. And that is the choice we face: either we exist from who we are or are enslaved by the state and other asserters through the self.'

'We are in a struggle which will not just end when the limits to misrepresentation in the marketplace have been reached rather the state to preserve itself will tighten the law of self in other areas. We face further restrictions on the freedoms to be who we are and more means to get us to surrender to ourselves. However, the state is trapped because everything it can do short of controlling our environment, and therefore our thoughts compromises its claim on freedom and leads to struggle with us. And just as we have only a single choice so does it: either it continues to enslave us or ceases to exist. The only way out for the state is to give other asserters more means to control us while risking the possibility that they may replace it or some of them may demand the same means of control. This is the beginning of the end of the state.'

'The hole in the law of self has made control over our minds the most sought after thing,' passes on the solitaire's mind. 'The self is the means.'

He looks around in the darkness of the battlefield and rests his hand on the heavy cannon.

'We are at war with any and all asserters,' he says to himself. 'There are no truces or surrenders because of the inherent conflict between who we are and the self. The more we strengthen through the weakness on our minds the more the asserters will attempt to control us by controlling our environment. It is how it is and will be. The conflict between who we are and the self cannot be avoided just as our movement to greater strength cannot be stopped. We are all in a constant state of flux driven by the eternal dynamic of strength through weakness with the weakness now being the asserters' self-serving values and beliefs, like justice and goodness, and the truths of existence being *the* strength.'

I am existence!

What Do Barb Wires Mean?

'The failing of the asserters' systems of ideas is that they only have meaning within them,' the solitaire thinks. 'The superior system of ideas will correspond to the meaning of existence.'

'The less our ideas correspond to existence the more vulnerable, and therefore weaker, we will be.'

'It is to be trapped in one's inferior system of ideas to assume that our environment has to change in order for a new system of ideas to have more value than any other. The strongest system of ideas or truths of existence corresponds to any environment because it is existence that is the basis for everything. To earn the superior mind is to eliminate any disparity between our ideas and the realities of existence. To do this our values and beliefs must correspond to existence. It is to go beyond *ourselves* and the overvaluing of our minds by consciously becoming part of existence.'

'Though our task is to eliminate the asserters' values and beliefs, *and* replace them with the truths of existence, we must not eliminate them all at once or otherwise we will not be able to replace all of them which will make us susceptible to other inferior ideas. It is like the green gardener at last removing all the weeds by the roots and having nothing to plant so that other weeds naturally take deeper root beneath the open spaces where the old weeds were. The best method to avoid such an outcome is to replace what we eliminate before moving on. And that is how it must be! because greatness of mind or anything is earned only through effortless patience or an uncompromising absorption in our task until it is completed. It is to sacrifice everything and even our own existence to fulfill the eternal task of existence which is to strengthen the endless whole through strengthening the beings of who we are.'

'To demand accountability from our beings is to demand it from others. To strengthen our beings is to force others to strengthen. It is to be a powerful part of everything causing everything else.'

He stands on the hilltop with his arms folded, around the darkness of his mind, and above the eternal unfolding of his thoughts.

'I cannot leave the battlefield with the taste of the self's weakness,' the solitaire says to himself. 'The moment is now to strike while it is wounded and in retreat. To back away is to give it new existence.'

'If I try to strike it and fail, I will be lost in the darkness.'

'I am in the darkness now,' flashes on his mind. 'The self is slowly drawing me from who I am through an illusion of victory. I am not armed. To rush back into the battlefield is to be like a blind man rushing towards the edge of a cliff without knowing or a woodsman pursuing a ferocious animal with a weapon and without ammunition for it.'

'I must strengthen by further uncovering the truths of existence. These are my only means to overcome the self. To do anything other than exist is to be caught by the anti-existence, the self which bleeds beings while having no existence of its own.'

'I am at the fringe between the self and existence. I can feel the vast space ahead of me. To go forward is to eliminate the basis for the self and enter the flow of existence. There is nothing to fear. Yet, I can't make the step. I could almost reach into the realm of existence though I am hesitant because to enter it is to never be the same being. What does it mean? The self fears its existence. It's trying to make me believe I will lose control over who I am, and thus put my own preservation at risk.'

'The basis for existence is the eternal dependency of all beings. There is no freedom as we believe there is. Every being no matter how strong is dependent on all other beings for its existence. We are all in the endless whole and connected to each other by the dynamic of strength through weakness. There are no beings or things in themselves because they have no meaning in existence where everything causes everything else. To be a being in itself is to be beyond the eternal dynamic, and therefore to be a whole, unchanging thing devoid of existence. It is to be outside the eternal forces of existence which is a fiction created by the asserters to establish a sense of order by getting us to believe we are accountable ends. Do we need proof to ease the uncertainty caused by our herd instinct? I ask us could we exist on our own without any need for anything else because that is what it means to be a being in itself? The reality is that we are dependent on our strength and the weakness of others which is why moving to greater strength is difficult. We are in an endless struggle with all other beings to exist through each other.'

'Our every breath requires an exertion of strength on our part to be able to inhale and utilize the weakness of the air, and our every thought is contingent on our effort to build off the weakness of others. Added to our struggle is that the weak do almost everything they can to preserve themselves by preventing us from strengthening through them. To break through weakness on any level is to contract the endless whole closer to the power of existence or in other words, to demand a higher standard for earning existence, and thereby *strengthen* our means to exist.'

'Already our existence requires constant earned effort on our part to just survive. To raise the standard is to force the weak to strengthen or face losing their existence, and those of them that strengthen will force us to strengthen even further or face losing our own existence. We are in a struggle that is coming at us from all sides as though lines of barb wire are winding and crisscrossing all around us. To move we have no choice, and to do so is to get constantly slowed down and snagged by the barbs. We don't notice the constant stabs or know any difference because there is nothing else. Where is our freedom I ask those that claim it's the meaning of their existence? Our every motion whether we are advocates of invented freedom or not is to be met with resistance from the barbs of every other being trying to survive and forces of nature which ensures we do not move unless we have to.'

'We are all in the barbs of existence whether we are aware of them or not, and it doesn't matter what we do to protect ourselves because we

will always be getting stabbed and snagged on one form of them or
another. To cease all movement including our breath is merely to change
our beings into another form while still existing in the barbs. To
strengthen our being is to get snagged less often than otherwise. It is to
be like an animal with thick fur existing in extreme winter conditions or
a being who thinks for himself while existing in an environment where
misrepresentation is the norm.'

I am *existence*!

What Do Wire Cutters Mean?

'Strength to persevere, to stay true to who we are admist weakness
and other strength is the meaning of our existence,' the solitaire says
himself. 'It is the mysterious power, and yet we all know it is the only
thing that truly distinguishes one being from another. We don't talk
about it rather we whisper about it when we bear witness to it in another
being. It is our secret, and therefore weakness, because it alone can make
us accountable. To exist by it is to break through the controls and lies of
our world, and render them meaningless because it is not the invention
called *me*, but only the power inside each of us that has meaning.'

'We do not face an impossible riddle to solve or even need to answer
the questions of how and why should we act. There are no riddles or
questions about our existence because we are already existing which is
the entire meaning of existence and our being: the eternal movement to
greater strength admist all other beings doing likewise, and it never
stops. It is to move to greater power and control over our beings, and
therefore over the weakness on and around us. Strength, which is the
basis for our existence, is the ability to say No to the weak or destroy
them, and ignore other strong or at most defend ourselves against them.'

'What is it?' the solitaire asks himself. He presses his hand against
his chin. 'I can't release myself and uncover the elusive force of
existence in me. The self is holding on while I try to wrench it lose, and
it cries the fear of death. It is death which still lingers on my mind as a
gruesome mask over the self. What does it mean? To overcome the self
is to overcome who I am? If there is no self what is there? How can I

72

exist without having any identity? Without the self I am still a being except that I am an eternally changing being. There is no self or identity for who I am because who I am does not exist as a concrete or absolute form. I am moving through existence while guided by a force inside. I have no control over who I am rather it is the changing force inside me that is guiding who I am through other changing forces doing the same. The self and death have no meaning except as labels to define what cannot be defined or to give meaning to eternal *changing* states of being which can never really be given meaning. And what is the meaning of strength I ask myself in our fleeting and changing existence? Are we afraid? We must be strong, and to be strong is to survive.'

'Strength is endless abilities to recognize weakness in ourselves and others for what it is, and thus avoid, withstand, overcome, or eliminate it. It is to surrender our minds and bodies to who we are, and beyond to the power of existence, and thereby move from the dynamic of changing strengths through changing weaknesses.'

The solitaire reenters the battlefield and aims the heavy cannon. The infantry stand nearby and ready.

'By becoming the changing force of our being we do not then earn the freedom to exist rather we earn the *strength to exist*.' He fires a volley and lowers his sword as the infantry to advance. 'The idea of freedom is not even a fantasy because to be free implies that somebody has given or allowed us to be free which is a form of control. In our illusory fantasy the concept of freedom always proceeds the qualifier *if* we meet certain conditions while in existence strength and nothing else, and with no qualifiers determines the degree we move from who we are. To get behind the idea of freedom is to disclose others trying to control us through the self, and to get behind the idea of strength is to face the power of existence in all of us.' The infantry converges on the enemy. 'To be free is to be something in itself acting as it wants though there is no something in itself, and therefore there are no so-called wants that come with it. Freedom is an imaginary state that distracts us, through the self, from existing who we are. It is to be snagged by weakness or barbs of existence while believing it to be something else or to spend our existence trying to attain more of it, and believing that we are while there has never been anything to attain. To be believe in freedom is a sickness of our mind and being because it is to be guided by the idea of weakness to exist rather than strength to exist. Instead of avoiding and cutting through barbs of existence with earned strength from sensing and knowing weakness the believers of freedom get snagged and more snagged by it, and at the same time convince themselves that it is freedom because it just has to be. They are like wind-up dolls except it is their minds and diets not cranks and springs which are bumping them aimlessly into things and each other.'

'Are we sensitive to others pointing out our weakness or is it the self making us feel sensitive? It is the call to be strong by taking command and control of our own minds! and the only way is to enter our battlefields armed with the question, what does it mean? and the power of the threesome force. To back away is to sink further into the nothingness of the self. To advance is to cut through self's disguises and the self itself. This is where our strength begins by accounting for the ideas on our minds and controlling the ones that enter them. It is to eliminate the asserters' mind cranks and exist from who we are. 'Enough!' is the thunder from our cannons. The more we advance the more the self tries to deceive us, but we are fearless and armed. 'What does it mean?' are the voices from the battlefields. There is panic and confusion on our side, and now a retreat. We have been fooled again. The self itself is a disguise for our belief in the thoughts on our consciousness which are inner perceptions of existence according to values and beliefs of the asserters. We are controlled by the asserters through the basis of our minds which are the values and beliefs which determine the general meaning of our thoughts. However, there is a way out by replacing the values and beliefs of asserters with the values and beliefs of existence, and thereby changing the fundamental basis for which we define and perceive our thoughts. For instance, our names or nouns will mean not beings in themselves, but eternal *changing* states of being, and our verbs or actions will not be causes or results, but parts of everything causing everything else. To move towards this is to move towards existing from who we are. It is to reduce our conflict and struggle with our minds by making the basis for them closer to the basis for existence.'

'The conflict and struggle with our minds is dangerous because it is *between* existing from who we are and not existing from who we are. We must not mistake that when we enter our minds through introspection we are entering the occupied space of others, and it is only by exerting from who we are that we make it into a battlefield. We must act against the asserters who are trying to plan and control our existence, and thereby deny us the unpredictability of our instinct, and therefore our adaptability. To let our existence be controlled and planned by them or anybody is to dampen our fire of strength through weakness or what makes us tenacious and strong. We become bored and eventually complacent and vulnerable from not acting our will to exist. It is like having somebody create plans for the construction of a house and expect and demand us to build it exactly as has been planned or having somebody make a detailed outline for a book and demand us to write it exactly as has been conceived, and the only difference being that we are dealing not with houses or books, but with *our* existence.'

'It has already been planned scientists tell us as they marvel at their latest fabrication called genetics. These are the deniers of existence who attach to their self-serving systems of thoughts which have no meaning in existence itself, and now they want to manipulate the basis for our existence. Genetics itself is a symbol for a perception and nothing more of the seeds of our beings which does not mean it is a blueprint or plan for our existence! It is merely a fictitious starting point for our physical beings in existence where action is the essence of moving. However, the scientists and other asserters want us to believe our own existence has been planned, and thus control us by *denying* the importance and even reality of our will to exist. To increase their control they have begun attempts alter the biological basis for our beings which requires access to our so-called building blocks or seeds, and therefore physical control over us. Similar to other asserters they do this by first controlling our minds, and then our bodies. However, no matter how much they alter our seeds they will never be able to manipulate the basis for who we are though they *can* impair the physical and mental means for us to exist it.'

'Our struggle is against those who try to control and plan our existence, and thus deny and suppress who we are instead of existing their own existence for themselves. Our strength comes from instinctual action which is the center and meaning of our existence. For our own preservation and the integrity of existence we must account the asserters of mediocrity who are afraid to exist for themselves. They are a weakness; and we are more a weakness if we are deceived into not acting against them.'

I am existence!

What Do Dynamites Mean?

'Our instinct is like dynamite because it has the potential for explosive strength contingent on whether we act upon it *or* the fuse is lit,' the solitaire reflects. 'The basis for it is a pure concentration of the dynamic of strength through weakness which is the meaning and force behind our drive to greater strength. Our minds and bodies' only function is to be mere extensions of it.'

'Behind the dynamic of strength through weakness itself is the power of becoming: the will to strengthen. The will is the dynamic or drive to exist, and the force behind it is pure power or *strength* in its most concentrated form. The only meaning of our existence is to strengthen, and to do this we must strengthen through weakness. There is no other way. This work itself is a form of weakness which we have the opportunity to strengthen through just as semen has the opportunity to strengthen through the weakness of beings' impulse to reproduce. Not all weaknesses will strengthen us just as not all strengths will result in more strength. We are in a struggle between endless, changing strengths where what may appear to be a weakness such as a book written for money or fame is an extension of the author's strength who is feeding off our weakness; and what may appear to be a strength such as a book written for a profound subject is both an extension of the author's strength through the weaknesses in the subject, and an extension our strength through him in which we all stand to strengthen.'

'Instinct is our means of survival because it gives us the power to sense the true strength of things, and thereby avoid being bled by other strengths or missing an opportunity to strengthen through a genuine weakness.'

FREEDOM FANTASY

'Though the meaning of existence is to become stronger it does not mean we strengthen for the sake of strengthening. We strengthen through our instinct, and therefore the weakness of our inner power which has a drive to become stronger according to the strengths and weaknesses of our being and in relation to all other beings who are doing the same thing. Nothing can exist without having weakness to feed off. Therefore to eliminate our false beliefs and perceptions of the *self* is to eliminate the self just as to eliminate our false views of books written for money or fame is to eliminate these books. All beings including ourselves are the weakness of everything that exists, and therefore the weakness or strength of whether they continue to exist.'

The solitaire stands on the hilltop overlooking the ruins of the battlefield. 'The will to power is nothing more than an expansion of the will to strengthen,' he says to himself. 'The will to power!' The infantry move towards him and listen.

'The basis for any social organization,' he declares, 'comes down to whether our will to have power over our own existence extends to having power over others as well. In the world there are no boundaries for strengths where they are endlessly unfolding by either joining or fragmenting into lesser or greater strengths. The force behind it is a mixture of strength through weakness and strength exploiting weakness *or* the strong ruling, controlling, and eliminating the less strong. Everything around us are endless strengths whose only purpose is to become stronger through weakness; and to believe otherwise is to be *already* exploited by some of them. Strengths like the asserters of mediocrity exploit many of us by getting us to strengthen to their advantage while making it partly to our advantage or appear to our advantage. They use us merely to cleanup after their explosions of inner dynamite, or in other words they get weakness to bleed other weakness. Though we may strengthen through the asserters it is negated because we make others weaker, and therefore ourselves weaker while denying ourselves an existence from who we are. In most cases, we are mere extensions of their will to strengthen in which they give us part of their loot for our sweat although other asserters and even themselves try to take it from us. Outside the fabricated world of asserters trying to convince us that they are reality, and thereby exploit us, existence controls everybody and nobody at the same time.'

'How can there be unity or harmony in existence when everything is strengthening through everything else?' the solitaire asks himself. 'It is chaos. To be a warrior of existence is to be warrior against everything else. There is no common ground except in the drive to strengthen. Is it possible to have unity from something that is inherently disunited?'

In almost a single, *one* movement the infantry move closer.

'The greatest unity results in the greatest strength,' he says. 'Is the greatest strength from the few exploiting the masses of weakness as the asserters would like us to believe? This is not unity of strength rather it is unity of mass exploitation by the few. They are strengthened and the masses are weakened which equates to not more overall strength, but more overall weakness. It is the idea of self behind this tragic idea of how to produce the greatest individual strength because only by overcoming the self do we realize that we are only as strong as each other.'

'The greatest unity and therefore the greatest strength is not from masses of weakness, but from the *oneness* of our will to strengthen as an endless whole. It is to surpass the illusory ideas of self, caste, aristocracy, race, and species, and exist united in the meaning of existence where our only purpose is to strengthen through weakness. Our power lies in the unity of our sole commitment to strengthen our beings, and therefore everything else. We have no attachments except for existing the power within us, and thus are able to see through the disguises of weakness to weakness itself. It is to be united by the will to strengthen though we act from the power within each of us. We are an unstoppable force because we work as a whole without appearing to work as a whole.'

'The basis for any social organization is in conflict with the union of purpose between all beings because the beings behind it utilize our strengths for the strength of their organization rather than for the strength of everything. Hence, to strengthen for anything other than the eternal whole of existence is to be in the control of other beings strengthening through us for their own advantage.'

'The power is inside all of us to fulfill the meaning of our existence which is the power inside us. We must not be deceived by believing that our strength is from the circularity of power. Our strength is from the *becoming* of power within us which is the invincible force of all our beings as a whole.'

I am existence!

What Do Fuses Mean?

'I want to leave the cave,' passes on the solitaire's mind. A tear trickles out his eyes as he glances at darkness.

'It's hard, but I must continue,' he says to himself. 'The will to power has to be earned. To give up now is merely to wound the asserters rather than hit them with a fatal blow. What does it mean? The self is distracting me which means I am near more weakness.'

'We have been hasty in our attacks on the asserters. We have been going after their weakness, and even been deadly accurate in our strikes, but we can do better. The battlefield itself needs to be studied so we can be both accurate and all encompassing in our strikes, and eventually take command of it and hold it.'

'The central element of our consciousness is *perception* just as blood is the central element of our body, and the will to strength is the central element of our being.'

'Every thought, memory, or imagination of our consciousness is contingent on there having been perceptions. To perceive is the same thing as to move for our bodies and to will for our beings; and just as we move and will endlessly forward and at all moments, we perceive endlessly forward and at all moments. Our movement is from space to space, our perception is from comparison to comparison, our will is from strength to strength. The basis for our space is other beings and their bodies, the basis for our comparisons is values and perceptions of other beings, the basis for our strengths is weakness and the existence of other beings. We are in an endless whole where everything not only causes everything else, but is dependent on everything else. There is no escape from our continuous moving and strengthening just as there is no escape from our continuous perceiving. We cannot get outside our bodies, consciousness, or beings. It is to be in an endless whole made up of smaller wholes or to be in a single, endless whole coming from a single will to strengthen. This is how we must perceive consciousness itself as either a scatter of different perceptions coming from the values and beliefs of others or a single, endless perception coming from our will to strengthen. We know and feel the power of the latter though the question is whether we have the strength to become it.'

The solitaire looks through a rising mist at the battlefield.

'It is appearances of perceptions which are just appearing and disappearing, and with ones always following. There is nothing else except for the appearances of them. To perceive our consciousness or anything is just to have another appearance of a perception on our consciousness.'

'Our minds are appearances of perceptions which are based on comparison of one or more appearance of perception with one or more other appearance of perception. There is no such thing as a perception itself because we cannot *perceive* a perception. We can only perceive an appearance of a perception. Nevertheless, there is order to our minds because when we perceive an appearance of a perception we believe it is a perception; and we have appearances of perceptions we call definitions and rules about our other appearances of perceptions, or in other words a system of appearances of perceptions from the appearances of perceptions.'

'The whole basis for how we perceive appearances of perceptions is from appearances of perceptions about appearances of perceptions. Any systematization of them is the control or will to strengthen, through appearances of perceptions, over how we perceive other appearances of perceptions. There is no truth, knowledge, thought, perception, imagination, memory, value, and belief except within a systematization of appearances of perceptions; and with *no* other meaning behind it except the will to strengthen.'

'For there to be any systematization of our perceptions we must be dishonest by labeling and defining what we have no basis to label and define except through an impulse to strengthen. It is to impart meaning to our minds when there is no basis to do so except that we do it. Our incentive to impart as much meaning as we can which is what some of the asserters have done by claiming that the basis for our minds is virtue, fairness, justice, soul, and spirit. These labels are nothing more than an attempt by the asserters to impart value to our minds themselves when there is none, and thereby justify their system of appearances of perceptions and control through it.'

'Those who control through anything other than their own being will do everything they can to protect through unreal elevation what they depend on for control such as the religious with their fictitious omnipotent Gods, and all other asserters with the invented virtuous mind. However, every system of appearances of perceptions including the will to strengthen is a *means* to control others. Though we can distinguish between them based on the source of the control and its effect on others. Is there an overvaluation of the will to strengthen as with other system of appearances of perceptions? Is the will to strengthen merely an attempt to control rather than a way to connect us to the power of existence in all us? We must decide for ourselves because there is no way of knowing except through our own appearances of perceptions.'

'My only justification for the will to strengthen is our instinct which I believe is the basis for our control over appearances of perceptions although it is also an appearance of perception. Again it comes down to deciding for ourselves which system of appearances of perceptions is the most true to who we are. Can there even be a choice when the others deprive us of being who we are whereas the will to strengthen produces the greatest unity and therefore the greatest strength through the independence of our beings and oneness of them? We don't choose to exist as a single will to strengthen we earn it by overcoming weakness, and thereby become our whole being's strength.'

The solitaire returns his view to the battlefield itself.

'If there are only changing appearances of perceptions where do they come from?' he asks himself. 'We have no way of knowing because all we perceive are appearances of perceptions of other appearances of perceptions. To believe they only come from our minds is to discount the influence of things outside our minds; and to believe they come from outside our minds is overlook the ability of our minds to produce its own appearances of perceptions. The mind is like anything else where everything causes everything else. In order to have appearances of perceptions and compare them we must have appearances of perceptions outside our minds to perceive while being able to compare them inside our minds. We can never produce appearances of perceptions from only our minds.'

'Through the reappearance of our appearances of perceptions themselves there appears to be a subconsciousness which produces and contains our appearances of perceptions. So our consciousness is appearances of perceptions coming from a subconsciousness which we know of by matching our appearances of perceptions with previous appearances of perceptions, and thus associating the subconsciousness with our ability to remember and compare them.'

'We are the sole authority over our minds because every appearance of perception whether it is from us or not is contingent on our appearance of perception of it. Though we lose control over our minds if we perceive how others want us to perceive our appearances of perceptions.'

'Since we can't get beneath our consciousness our control over it comes from control of our appearances of perceptions. We must make them accountable through the application of our instinct, and establish our own beliefs and values. To do otherwise is to allow appearances of perceptions of others influence our actions and lessen our ability to exist who we are. However, we cannot just wish them to happen because they will not. We must take control over our appearances of perceptions which is to use our mind as a tool rather than let others dictate our existence through it.'

'To think is to take control over our subconscious comparisons of appearances of perceptions, have the ability to scrutinize any appearance of perception. As with any movement thinking is a will to strengthen which does not happen of its own doing rather we must exert our consciousness over both appearances of perceptions and the system of fabricated beliefs and values behind them. The only purpose of thinking is to strengthen our minds by eliminating weakness on it, and decide through the guide of our instinct our actions against external weakness. Our challenge is to avoid getting trapped in others' systems of appearances of perceptions while believing that we are thinking from our instinct. To avoid this we must scrutinize beliefs and values as they manifest themselves in our appearances of perceptions. It is to perform at a shooting-range except the gun is our thinking, the being holding it is our will to strengthen, and the target is others' appearances of beliefs and values behind appearances of perceptions appearing and disappearing on our minds.'

I am existence!

What Do Explosions Mean?

'I can't take anything serious now,' the solitaire says to himself. 'Everything is and always will be from the will to strengthen, and yet most of us deny it because we are either already trapped by the asserters' systems of appearances or are the ones behind it.'

'How far have I fallen?' he asks. 'Was my assent to the summit of existence only an appearance on my mind?'

He motions his hands through the darkness of the cave.

'Is this what our perceptions are like on our minds except we pretend they have meaning? The baseness of our existence,' the solitaire reflects. 'All things to us will always be nothing more than an appearance of a perspective. Even the appearance is in doubt because it may just be an illusion on our minds which only has meaning through a system of illusions, thereby making our existence even more powerless. We are like blind beings who think they can see, and if you try to tell them they call you insane.'

'The meaning of the summit has returned,' he says to himself. 'It only has meaning if we all earn the assent.' He opens his eyes to the darkness as a tear edges down his cheek.

'Our existence would not be so disgusting if we were not so dishonest about it. We can't do that because the asserters would lose their control over our minds, and therefore over our existence. The only hope for us is to strengthen through the asserters and beyond to where we all exist from our own will to strengthen. It is to be strong from becoming one-beings.'

83

WHAT DO EXPLOSIONS MEAN?

'I have the strength to say this because I have earned the power of perspective from deep inside me *and* everywhere to say it,' the solitaire confesses to some and therefore all. 'I am stronger than any of the asserters because my followers are stronger than anybody else! Ask *yourself* what grounds you have to think I am a madman, and I don't mean just ask, but get into your shooting-range and blast both the appearance of self and the mad self, and maybe even question your integrity for believing two of the asserters' appearances of fabricated beliefs. And for those who sense my courage and strength, and have enough of their own strength to know it is not me, but the power of existence through my being which gives me strength consider this:

> We must *act* to strengthen.
> To act we must have strength.
> We need strength to strengthen.

Power! Our reality is that we must come from the power of strength because it is the basis for action which is the basis for everything. We cannot exist without the action to move, think, or will, and therefore without the strength to move, think, or will. There is no beginning to strength because there is no appearance of anything in itself or beginning to anything.'

'The question facing our existence is whether we act from the will to strengthen from our own being or others' beings. This has never been an issue, but I am making it one! by exposing all of us for what we are and showing a way to be who we are. We must not mistake that it is a weakness to exist off the strength of others rather than strengthening from our own being. The notion of strengthening by using some in order to exploit many others is destructive. It is to strengthen through the weakening of almost everything else whereas in hard reality everything is only as strong as everything else. Am I a defeatist or perhaps *I am right* in saying that there are limits to strengthening through action, and that in many circumstances non-action leads to more strength than action? However, nothing will come of this unless we act because we are the mediocre basis for the asserters' existence. To strengthen ourselves is to weaken them, and to become one-beings is to eliminate their systems of mind control and force them to exist for themselves.'

'The greatest strength is from each of us earning our existence for ourselves,' the solitaire reflects. 'I can sense our fear for doing what we have almost never done which is to act from who we are. However, I am not asking us to confront the beings behind the asserters rather I am informing us that confronting their fabricated beliefs and values on our minds is the only place to begin our will to strengthen. All it requires is for us to get into our shooting-range and pull the trigger on our instinctual thinking.'

'Though we have the highest objective of attaining a state where everyone earns their existence without the *help* of others, and therefore through the greatest help of all, no help! this is a far-off powerful state of being which we can only earn through each explosion of our will to strengthen. It is not just explosions from within rather we have to have control of them, and thus use them to move us closer to our objective and nothing else. We always have the shooting-range of our consciousness to account for all appearances of fabricated beliefs and values, and the hole in the law of self through which we can share our earned strength with those worthy.'

'Our challenge is to persevere within the numerous constraints on who we are by saving our explosive fire for where it counts: against the creators of mediocrity. To eliminate the asserters through a global annihilation of their fabricated values and beliefs is to eliminate all other mediocrity, and yet to get drawn into confrontation with mere beings of mediocrity is to risk wasting our existence by not furthering our objective as much as we could. We must be focused on our task admist masses of weakness trying to distract us from it, and therefore be selective in how we utilize our power from within. It is to control our explosions by controlling our fuses instead of letting others misfire us. The reality is that our explosions are *only* as powerful as our focus on the highest objective.'

'We must not confuse that we earn our strength from both acting and not acting which can only happen by having control over who we are. Our greatest and only challenge is to act from our beings. To do this we must use our disgust for the things we feel and see to strengthen who we are. It is to strengthen through the sickness of others and their abuse and ridicule by ignoring it and responding through our own inner strengthening and saving our power for where it counts most, and to do otherwise by unnecessarily harming anybody is to misuse our power and give the mediocre cause to strengthen through us. We must be strong and contain our earned pride by avoiding them and even if necessary backing away from an encounter with them. The highest objective must not be compromised. To be strong and thereby give the mediocre nothing to strengthen through is to force them to strengthen through themselves and each other! In other words, our strength shifts the focus to where the weakness really is which is to let the mediocre destroy themselves by themselves while allowing us to concentrate on overcoming the asserters' fabricated beliefs and values, and replacing them with the truths of existence. Strength is the exclusive force that determines everything, and there is only one way to earn it: by acting from the power of who we are. Those truest to who they are will persevere, and thus strengthen everything else. However, there are no winners and losers or victors and defeated because we all strengthen through ourselves and each other. We cannot be stopped because it is the natural movement of everything to strengthen; and so in that sense there are no divisions between beings rather there are differences in changing strengths which are all moving to the power of existence.'

I am existence!

What Do Self Bombers Mean?

'Do I have any followers?' the solitaire laughs to himself. 'They are the weak who have been drawn from their own beings and into the power of others. To produce and depend on followers is a sickness of a human being's mind just as to follow others is a negation of the meaning of a human being's existence. Nobody is or has ever been worthy of being followed.'

'Am I no different from the producers of followers? My objective, the highest objective has been to produce strong and independent beings by myself becoming one of the strongest and most independent beings. It is to demand a higher standard for existence through increasing and sharing the strength of my own being with those worthy. And yet how can I reconcile helping to strengthen others when letting others earn their own existence not only leads to the greatest strength, but is the basis for my beliefs? Again I ask do I have any followers and add, is there any being to follow? I am not helping others because they need the strength to understand my thoughts and put them to action for themselves though I am doing what others could do themselves, and if they did they would be that much more stronger. However, does it make sense for all of us to instinctual think through the meaning of our existence when one of us could do it and share it with all of us? Feel the *weakness* of this idea which is the basis for civilization! My existence is not ideal though its power and meaning is from working towards the highest objective by giving others the means to strengthen through the weakness I strengthened through. It is to work away from the rotten core of our world and to the purity of existence, and the only way to do it is to gradually strengthen through the idea of societal dependency. To expect us to just become strong, independent beings by merely wanting it is like thinking strength comes from following others. We must earn each and every step towards the becoming-man. And mistake not my work is not a handout. It is only for the truly strong because it is only them who have the strength and courage to overcome themselves, and thereby earn the power of existence through my instinctual thoughts.'

'Followers like anything else thrive off weakness except they thrive off not the weakness of what is produced, but the weakness of those who produce it. For this to occur there must be *separation of being* between the producer and what is produced to allow an opening for the followers to exploit the producer as opposed to facing a single mirror of who we all are. Money or fame does not determine the integrity and strength of anybody; it is whether they have any followers or not, and if they do *how many*. The more followers there are the more there is lack of unity and therefore integrity between the producer and what is produced, and thus the halves themselves.'

'The greatest beings and works are those that do not produce followers, but stronger beings. How do they do it? They earn it through *pain* because it is only through overcoming weakness and the struggle

and effort to do it that we truly strengthen. And for that reason we must
return to our work at hand.'

'Our greatest weakness is also our greatest strength. It is our
imaginary belief in the existence of the self. Our focus on the asserters'
fabricated values and beliefs must inevitably converge on it for us to
strengthen by becoming who we are. As it stands, the self is like a dam
regulating the flow of our will to strengthen and will continue to do so
until we instinctually think through it. To do this is to release the power
of our own beings in which *everything* on our minds, and therefore
around us becomes accountable. Though even by doing this we would
still perceive through the self.'

The solitaire glances towards the opening of the cave.

'I don't know how to overcome the self,' he confesses to everyone
and no one. 'My struggle and pain has been almost without meaning
unless I can pull it out by the roots and have something to replace it
with.'

He edges further into darkness.

'What is the idea that will just alter the appearance of everything we
perceive?' passes on his mind.

His hand touches the wall at the end of the cave.

'To realize there is no being or anything in itself is not enough to
overcome the self. It has been tried by many without success. The only
thing that can do it is existing from our will to strengthen though we can
only do that by overcoming the self. The secret is to not deny or detach
ourselves from the self, but to think and act for ourselves. To react or try
to overcome the self is to be already trapped by it because our actions
are giving it existence which it would not have. And that is the point: we
have only so much existence which the self and all its offspring, the
asserters and marketplace *drain* from us as the only basis for their
existence. Therefore for us to merely exist from who we are is to
overcome them all. It is to give them no existence by having the strength
to avoid and stay clear of them, and thus force the beings behind them to
earn their existence for and by themselves. The negation of the being in
itself is powerful though for it to have meaning we must act! We have
been mislead by the association of the self with the imaginary ego when
in essence the self is nothing more than a denial of the will to strengthen.

The question we must ask ourselves is what do our actions mean? Are we acting to strengthen others through our*selves* or are we acting to strengthen our whole being? The danger we face is getting trapped by the masses of mediocrity who are making the self and its offspring a basis for our existence. What are we conforming to and why? and again we sense our weakness for *not* acting from who we are. I don't want to hear any excuses because we all know inside us that there is something wrong with conforming to what is making all of us weaker beings. We must be strong by seeing the large picture in which the asserters are trying to make their self-serving reality the standard for our existence, and the only way for them to do it is to get most of us to conform to them, and thereby give them *control* over our existence. The only way out is for us to strengthen through the weakness on our minds.'

He presses the palm of his hand against his forehead.

'I must keep moving,' he says to himself. 'The cave is only so deep, but the will to strengthen is endless and so is strength.'

'The becoming-man,' flashes on his mind.

I am existence!

NEEDS DECEPTION

What Do Worlds As Lie Mean?

'To move beyond the weakness of our minds is to never return as we are,' the solitaire says to some, and therefore all.

'We exist in a fictional world where to truly strengthen ourselves is actually to weaken ourselves in relation to the masses of mediocrity. To do as the herd is to deny our existence and to do as we are meant to be is to risk our existence. We can't strengthen only part way through our minds because this is what the masses use against us. We must strengthen all the way through them, and thereby make us an *impenetrable* strength. It is to become our existence while making the masses strengthen their own through each other or face losing it.'

'What does it take to exist the elusive will to strengthen and even when we know it is the only thing worth striving for? Instead we struggle through weakness after weakness or are trapped by others' exploitation while believing we are strengthening from ourselves. The hard reality is that we must earn our strength regardless if we know it or not. *Every upward step we make must be through our own blood.* To ascend through the exploitation of the masses is to be elevated for only as long as it continues, and for that reason the asserters will do everything they can to hold onto what they have. Our time will come when we strengthen beyond them, and meanwhile we must be steadfast in strengthening our beings. It is to gradually become the power of existence.'

He faces the darkness of the cave and perceives the appearances on his mind.

'Everything to us is through appearances of perceptions and their invented meanings. Outside our minds, our appearances have meaning only in that they are based on what we perceive existence to be or what others want us to perceive it to be, and on our minds they only have meaning within systems of them. Since all meaning is based on inventions there is no such thing as meaning itself rather meaning is just an extension of an invention which only has meaning itself as an invention and nothing else. In other words, everything on our minds is a form of fiction with meaning only within the fiction itself, and therefore our existence, at least our perception of it, is nothing more than a fiction which we invent. However, our instinct tells us there has to be more! and there is because to invent requires strength and strength itself requires a will to strengthen.'

'Everything to us through our minds and thus our senses is a will to strengthen which correlates to not the appearance of existence, but the basis of it. What we sense is contingent on what we believe we sense rather than sensing what is actual because what is actual does not exist. Our senses *do not* directly translate into ideas or images on our minds. Instead our minds process them through a system of appearances on our subconscious. It is to give us power over our minds because our system of appearances must correlate to our senses, like what we smell or touch, to have a semblance of meaning unless we allow ourselves to become controlled by the system and its meanings for our senses. The asserters can never have control over our minds except if either we allow them or they control our environment which they can never do. Our ability to sense not only around us and the appearances on our minds, but also our will to strengthen makes us powerful beings. It gives us the means to scrutinize the system of appearances on our minds and to create our own system of appearances.'

'The challenge facing us is to create our own system of appearances of perceptions so that it matches our sensory information of existence. The critical step is determining what we actually sense without being influenced by other systems of appearances, and as I have maintained sensing, and if need be scrutinizing what we sense, through our instinct or the power of who we are is only way to do this because it is to strengthen not for our fictitious *self*, but for everything through strengthening our own beings.'

'Though we cannot get away from inventing the appearances on our minds, we can make them resemble as closely as possible what we sense and the meaning of the appearances of what we sense through our instinctual honesty. Even if we do this we cannot get away from the reality that everything on our minds is an invention, and the only difference between them being how true they are to what we instinctually sense which we will never know except by instinctually sensing what we instinctually sense. What this means is that honesty is not something that can be created or learned rather it can only be existed because it is the basis for who we are! The more honest we are the more accurate will be the meaning we give to the appearances of what we sense, and to have a more accurate appearance of perception of existence than others is to be stronger than they are because we will be in a better position to respond to the actuality of things around us. We must not confuse that being honest within others' system of appearances on our mind may be to act with *less* honesty than we are capable because honesty comes only from who we are and not what others want us to think. Yet regardless of how honest we are we must invent the meaning of our appearances of perceptions which leads me to ask: is our existence and the world nothing more than lies which we can only claim to have the most honest lies?'

'For us to lie there must be truth to lie about, and since there is no truth because every appearance of perception on our minds is an invention there is no such thing as lie. The will to strengthen is the basis for an invention, and therefore it is the basis for our appearances of our existence and the world. *Instinctual honesty distinguishes one invention or strength from another with the more honest invention being the stronger*. The appearances of our existence and the world as lies is a denial of our existence *and* the world as strengths, and from some of us being trapped by the asserters' system of appearances.'

'Thou shall not lie! is an invented value the asserters use to get us to conform to their system of appearances of perceptions because without our conformity their system loses even its fictional meaning. The asserters' system of appearances is nothing more than many inventions built upon each other, and is similar to the self in that both of them depend on controlling us though they themselves have no existence except through controlling us. To see how absurd their system is before a judge we are required to tell the whole truth, and nothing but the truth as though there is *no* truth to tell. So to tell the truth as the asserters' demand is actually to be dishonest to who we are instead of acting out our will to strengthen, and thereby saying anything that would increase our strength. Their system of appearances is a contradiction because they expect us to not invent when the system itself and anything in it are inventions. However, beyond the obvious contradiction the system is about the will to strengthen of few over many which is condition as mentioned on the conformity of the many to the few. What kind of system of appearances has the basis for it that we weaken ourselves by telling the illusory truth instead of strengthening ourselves through the honesty of who we are? It is a fatal sickness of the whole system to expect us to act against our meaning which is to strengthen. The irony is that to exist beyond the requirement to tell the illusory truth is to become more honest to who we are, and thus strengthen through the asserters and their system of mind control. It is to reverse the scenario of who is controlling who though unlike the asserters our objective is to not control others rather it is to strengthen the eternal whole of existence through strengthening our own beings.'

'We have an onus on ourselves to not lie, because there is no such as lie, but to be honest to who we are. It is to instinctually think for ourselves instead of being trapped by the asserters' fabricated morals designed to control our existence through our minds. We must not confuse that the legal oath, I promise to say the whole truth, and nothing but the truth translates into I promise to be weak, and nothing but weak! Even if all of us conformed to saying the imaginary truth is that the kind of system of appearances we would want to be part of whereby we are expected to weaken ourselves rather than strengthen ourselves? It is be controlled by the beings behind the asserters because it is them and nobody else who invent the core imaginary truths which we would be conforming to. It is a fraud! and we will have no part of it. We don't demand a new system of appearances because all systems of the mind are about the control of some over others, and at this moment we are in the endless of whole existence where there are no oaths and instead the single demand on all of us to strengthen! What more could we ask than to be part of something that just lets us be who we are? It is to go before a judge and say I promise to be a whole strength, and nothing but a strength, and not even this because we would just exist it. And that is power of existence where there are no controls over others except through the strength of who we are, and the asserters' system of appearances of perceptions is *merely one of those controls* which we have the strength not only to not conform to, but to overcome by increasing the strength of our beings.'

'To believe that we don't have the strength to overcome the asserters' system of appearances is to be already trapped in it rather than existing solely from who we are. Asking ourselves, 'what does our fear mean?' and then answering it with instinctual honesty can be our first upward step of strength.'

'In almost all of our experiences with ourselves and others there are opportunities for upward steps though we must act upon our instinctual awareness of them. We have the power to strengthen everything through strengthening our own beings though we must act from who we are for it to happen. It is to act with the will to exist, and more still with the *resolve* to do everything we can to ensure that we exist.'

I am existence!

What Do Quests For Truth Mean?

'It is a mistake of mine to believe that I can just tell others to strengthen their beings when the best and only way is to strengthen our *own* beings,' the solitaire thinks. 'Perhaps I am caught by the absurdity of our existence in which there is a need to tell others to strengthen for themselves! However, it is also an indication of how much control the asserters have over our minds and environment, and therefore our existence. For that reason maybe my thoughts are *not* nonsensical, but are a guide or even a reminder to us that our existence really has meaning.'

'We have become so weak through ourselves and the asserters; and it is from weakness in the asserters control over the many that they cannot prevent the increasing disparity between them and the many, and thus the exposure of their control over them and the resulting mediocrity. So it is not a mistake to tell us to strengthen because that is the level ourselves and the asserters have brought us to though as we know it is up to us *alone* to strengthen.'

'Will there come time when we will have to be reminded to walk or even breath?' he asks himself. 'We invented laughter so what is there to stop us from reinventing breathing?'

His eyes close on the darkness of the cave.

'Inventions only have meaning if we give them meaning by believing in them,' passes on his mind. 'Nothing on our consciousness has meaning unless we give it meaning. Instinctual honesty is the only way we have to distinguish one invention from another because unlike logic it goes beyond the inventions while being nothing more than an invention itself. We have appearances through sensing our instinct which we call instinctual honesty rather than experiencing them for themselves. It is our minds that are the traps because we can never be true to what we sense without having to invent appearances for what it means. So through my fictional symbol called instinctual honesty I believe we can sense the meaning of it, and what distinguishes the strength between us is those who act upon it more than others. Our strength is not just from acting upon honesty, but acting upon it amongst others acting upon it and trying to get us to not act upon it ourselves. Most times it happens so fast that we don't follow our instinct, and instead become a weakness which other beings strengthen through. Our resolve to exist, and thus resist others trying to strengthen through us, is the power from knowing that we are only as strong as each other and that we earn strength solely from existing for ourselves. It is to step beyond being guided by fabricated morals that both tell us to deny our existence and let others to strengthen through us by having clean minds.'

'I must be a madman for reinventing honesty while denying the existence of truth and non-truth. It is to claim to be honest, and yet have nothing to be honest about,' the solitaire says to himself. 'Though I say we ourselves are mad for believing the asserters' inventions instead of existing beyond them. The relevancy of any invention comes from how much it corresponds to existence, and for that reason I move beyond truth and non-truth, and honesty and dishonesty, and declare that there is only the honesty to strengthen. It is not weakness from feeling an obligation or duty to say the illusory truth rather it is the power to follow our will to strengthen admist others doing likewise. What distinguishes

95

our honesty from each other is the differences in our awareness of our impulses to strengthen.'

'To increase our strength is only honest in the sense that others perceive it as a challenge and threat to them without realizing that we are only as strong as each other. There is *nothing* honest about acting from who we are except that we exist in a world where to act from who we are instead of the asserters' system of appearances of perceptions is the exception rather than the norm. And that is the crux of our struggle in which the asserters want us to believe that the illusion of honesty comes from conforming to their system of appearances and us who believe it comes from being who we are. However, we must be stronger by moving beyond honesty, and into existence where everything is an unfolding will to strengthen. To cling to the invention of honesty as a justification for who we are is like holding onto somebody's arm for support when we don't need to. The person unnecessarily *influences* how we move just as the invention creates an extra step for us to exist our own beings. Our power is not from the honesty to strengthen; it is from strength.'

'Similar to honesty we have been fooled by truth itself in which many of us spend our short existence studying and learning for the sake of studying and learning or in a vain quest for truth. We do not exist for ourselves rather we search for meaning when everything we need to know is inside us. The tragedy is that we are not motivated by our will to strengthen, but the conscious inventions of the asserters. It is as though we are on a leash tied to a stake in which we move around and around while imagining that we are moving somewhere else except the leash is our appearances of perceptions, and the stake is the asserters' invented values like the virtue of knowledge behind our appearances. The values always move with us and us always around them as we *imagine* we are learning and coming closer to the truth of things. The reality is that there is nothing to learn or seek, and everything to strengthen. If we are not strengthening ourselves it means others are strengthening through us, and so we must ask ourselves why we sit in classrooms where most professors tighten our leash and reinforce the stake by tapping it further into the ground or why we travel to foreign lands to learn and discover as though there is something meaningful in doing such a thing!'

NEEDS DECEPTION

'The asserters glorify scientists or the discovers of their system
truths for no other reason than to keep us secured to the stake, and thus
from existing our own will to strengthen. They encourage us to learn and
seek through their system of appearances even though they know there
has never been nor will there ever be anything to seek or learn. The
challenge we face is not to do things for the sake of them or because the
asserters' false values induce us to do them, but to do them for the
increase strength of our whole being.'

The solitaire opens his eyes to the darkness of the cave.

'Everything we perceive through our consciousness and regardless of
how connected it is to our instinct is an invention. Truth is no different
from any other invention except the asserters use it to get us to conform
to their system of appearances by creating an illusion that the system and
its appearances of values and beliefs are real. The more we conform to
their system of appearances the more we are likely to believe that what
we perceive is real when in fact we are just perceiving through more and
more layers of inventions built on each other. It is only by getting
outside their inventions through other systems of appearances or
realizing the basis of them that we know there is nothing real on our
minds nor will there ever be except for appearances themselves.'

'Everything we perceive through our minds is the will to strengthen
through inventions; it is real, but not as what we think we perceive. We
may believe this is a book in front of us, and even call it a truth: there is
a book in front of us, though it really is a will to strengthen in the form
of an appearance on our minds *and* through other inventions. Truth or
the so-called real only exists as the will to strengthen, and therefore in
order to exist in the real we must identify the real for what it is rather
than what others want us to identify it as. So instead of believing for
instance we turned off a light and insist that it was on and now it is off,
we believe we acted and perceived through the inventions of other's will
to strengthen, and thus the light only turned off by us acting and
perceiving through a system of appearances which matches the
appearance of a light turning off. The light itself cannot be turned off
because it does not exist, and instead we can only imagine ourselves
turning it off. The will to strengthen itself does not exist either; it is an
invention.'

97

WHAT DO HARD REALITIES MEAN?

A tear edges down the solitaire's cheek.

'We will never know what is real because we do not know anything except by inventing. And yet we *do* because to never know what is real is real.'

I am existence!

What Do Hard Realities Mean?

'An invention is not real because it is a fabrication or an invention is real because it is an extension of what is real?' the solitaire asks himself. 'We will never know though we know that everything we perceive is just an appearance of an invention.'

'Since invention itself is an invention, and an invention or anything has no existence in itself what is behind it? To invent we must have strength to exist or to make our existence into something it would not be otherwise. We are the creators of our existence in which we *must* invent in order to have meaning. To invent is to exist, and to exist is the will to strengthen. We can never get behind invention itself nor can we ever exist except by inventing in which everything outside of our appearances of inventions is nothing although we know inventions come from something. However, the something is critical because it determines the basis for all inventions even though it can only be an invention itself! And that is fitting because everything is an invention anyway and as we know invention itself is the means for us to exist, and therefore everything is the means to exist by being *unknown* which forces us to invent in order to exist. It is as if we were created in such a way as to earn our existence for ourselves! and thereby increase the strength of all beings through the increase strength of our own being. The unknown something behind everything, because it is unknown, is the force which ensures there will always be the need to invent and reinvent, and therefore to exist. Our struggle or opportunity centers around that there is *no* absolute invention, and hence all of them are the will to strengthen. All existing appearances of inventions can be and will be replaced by other appearances of inventions. Everything on our minds and around us through our minds is the will to strengthen through unfolding appearances of inventions.'

'World power revolves around the control of inventions by some beings preventing most beings from inventing for themselves or getting beings to invent for them. Those with the most power have control over the means to inventing or the inventions which the masses have been brainwashed into believing they want and need.'

'*All* invented values are a means to control inventions by getting us to act according to the inventions of others. It is to invent a system for how we should act and justify it through other inventions while having no basis for doing so except the will to strengthen through the appearances of inventions. The religious, through the invented omnipotent being, use the fabrications of altruism, compassion, kindness, honesty, love, equality, and self-sacrifice to get us to deny inventing for ourselves, and the state and money-makers, through the invented soul or spirit of the mind, use the fabrications of virtue, truth, fairness, and justice to justify their control of how we use inventions and get us to invent within their invented values and beliefs.'

'Without surprise, neither the religious nor the state and money-makers act from the invented values they push on us because there would be no invented values to push on us! Instead they act from a ruthless desire for self-preservation and the beliefs that they are only as strong as the weakness of others, and strength comes from existing through the weakness of others. All their appearances of invented values have no meaning in existence except as a means to strengthen through us, and even value itself is biased to what they invent as values.'

'We are uneasy because we have been indoctrinated with these fabricated values and habituated to them to such a point that we consider them part of who we are. We fear there is a void of nothingness without them when in reality there is a void of nothingness with them! They get us to deny the meaning of our existence which is to invent and use inventions to strengthen our *own* being.'

'Beyond invented values is the power of existence which is the guiding force of all beings. The will to strengthen, everything causing everything else, eternal *changing* states of being, eternal accountability, dynamic of strength through weakness, everything only as strong as everything else, and strength through existing for ourselves are invented truths describing existence. They do not control our existence rather they bring us consciously closer to reality which none of us can escape from. We must ask ourselves why we would be guided by anything other than the invented truths of existence since existence itself is the basis for everything?'

'All values for how we act and what we wear are not only a disguise for strength through weakness, but a means itself to strengthen through weakness. Everything around us in disguise or not is the will to strengthen. The strongest beings act from the power of existence through not the false values of others, but their *own* beings.'

The solitaire closes his eyes to the darkness of his mind, and then reopens them to the darkness of the cave.

'I can't do it,' he says.

'We exist in a reality where the only thing that is real is that everything is a fabrication. Why must we strengthen and endure the pain and struggle to do it? There are no answers. It is like we are on a journey in a dream without knowing where we are going, for how long, or why, and the only way to know is to *pretend* we know where we are going, for how long, and why. Is it insanity to believe we are in reality when there is no reality? We can't even pretend because pretend itself is an appearance of an invention, and *appearance itself is an appearance of an invention*. We are all in something, and we will never know what it is or what it means. What is *we* itself and in something? They are appearances of inventions. Everything including *everything* itself is unknown.'

'From this unknown we must invent our existence though we have no way of knowing what for, and therefore how. It is as though we are in a darken room without knowing where and what we are or anything at all, and someone asks us to tell him where and what we are. However, our situation is worse because we have appearances of a world which we know are fabrications and even know the appearance of our own being is a fabrication, and now someone asks us to tell him the meaning of our existence in the world. We respond, because there is no other response except a denial of what is, that our meaning is to exist fabrications in fabrications.'

'The question we face is how to use what we know or don't know as a basis for deciding why and how we exist. It would amount to an elimination of all values and beliefs except for those we choose to value and believe while knowing that they, and we as well, are mere fabrications.'

'The best we can do without becoming nothingness is to exist with the least fabrications rather than with the most as we do! and therefore at least, assuming a fabrication is a fabrication no matter what it is, we would exist closest to nothingness. The idea would be to use only the fabrications we need to sustain our existence while acting from our only belief that everything is nothingness.'

'We must pretend we are beings that need to be sustained, and then invent the means that will sustain us. Since everything is nothing we will never know what the least means are to maintain our beings, and therefore we will never escape the journey in the dream or the darken room.'

'Our danger lies in trying to invent our own reality which will move us further from the truth of existence and into more and more fabrications that do not even have meaning themselves. We may think that fabrications are nothingness anyway so it does not matter how many we use to structure our existence. They are though they also have meaning in relation to each other which eliminates the possible reality that there is *no* relationship between anything.'

'If existing in and as truth is the purest and strongest state of being we would do everything we can to maintain our connection to truth, and instead we exist in a world that is taking us, if we let it, further away from truth. The power of nothingness is that it is both the basis of everything, and something we can never escape from. The more connected we are to it the more we are able to avoid and even eliminate fabrications designed to control us. The modern world with all its fabrications is an attempt by some to separate us from the *power* of our only truth, and thereby control our existence. Almost all of us are acting fabrications within fabrications while pretending they and ourselves are real. It is a mistake which can only cease to be if most of us realize the imaginary relationship between fabrications.'

WHAT DO STRENGTHS AS ONLY NEED MEAN?

'The sole thing we can *trust* with our whole being is the emptiness of everything, and that does not mean there is no meaning rather there is no way we will ever know. It is nonsensical to not center our existence, as is the case with the world, around the only truth we know because to do so amounts to a *denial* of our reality.'

I am existence!

What Do Strengths As Only Need Mean?

'I have been mistaken. There is another truth,' the solitaire says to himself. 'Since everything is and will always be nothing we must invent or use inventions to exist. Even though we don't invent because invention is only an appearance on our minds, we must do something whatever we want to call it. It is to make something of the darken room while always being in it. So the reality of our existence is that we must do something, whatever that something is, in an existence where everything including ourselves is nothingness. Our challenge is to make something out of nothing without knowing what for or how and pretend the something we invent is actually something.'

'We return to the darken room, though we are in it right now! and imagine ourselves making up something from what we sense. We don't know why we sense or what it means except that we have senses without knowing that we do. What is our *first thought*, and most important, what is the meaning of it? We will never know what it is though we know that we made one which tells us that we made it to understand the unknowable from our own perspective, and therefore to strengthen our beings. The meaning of our first thought is the will to strengthen because to assert ourselves in the most innocent and threatening situation is to strengthen ourselves by making our situation less threatening. In the darkness we can only pretend to make something out of nothing just as there is only one reason we would do it which is to strengthen because whether we are conscious of it or not we are *strengthening* and nothing else. It is to face the continuation of our existence or not, and we respond in the most innocent way, because we don't know anything, as if by saying we don't care about nothingness we want to exist! We are courageous to enter the unknown and invent our existence while always remaining in the unknown. However, no matter how much we strengthen through inventing our existence we will be no more or less stronger because nothingness is and will always be the meaning of everything.'

'So we come back to our first thought and ask ourselves whether we should have made it or stayed true to the nothingness of existence by not inventing anything? Perhaps there is another existence we can only enter by becoming *nothing* rather than pretending to be something. It may be the ultimate test which we can only pass by being true to the meaning of everything. We don't know, although it appears to take more courage and strength to become what we are rather than pretending to be something we are not.'

'Nothingness must be the answer to all of existence, and we could be it and still invent by realizing the emptiness of the appearances on our minds. To realize and exist nothing we must deconstruct the appearances we have attached meaning to except for those we have attached the meaning of nothingness. It is to gradually work our way back to our first thought and make the basis for it and all of them emptiness.'

'It is nonsensical to work our way back to nothingness while pretending to be something we are not,' the solitaire reflects. 'Either we are something or nothing, and not both of them at the same time. To pretend there is existence when there is not is a *denial* of what is.'

'If we enter the unknown our existence as we know it will *end* though we do not know what will follow whereas if we invent our existence we will exist in a fiction which has connections between inventions *and* no meaning in existence. Our only way out is to blend the two paths by realizing the nothingness of everything while inventing and using inventions to sustain our existence. It will allow us to exist something, and be true to both nothingness and the possibility that there may be meaning behind it. Though we will never know what is behind nothingness unless we earn the strength to enter it.'

'Our challenge is to deconstruct and reconstruct our minds at the same time so that the basis for all our appearances is nothingness. It is to unite our minds with the rest of our beings and existence all around us, and thus become *one* with the emptiness of existence. We leave the darken room or wake up from the journey in the dream and consciously enter and *become* reality. Our whole beings flow with the power of existence rather than wearing ourselves out in the invented struggles created by ourselves and others. Our strength comes from existing nothingness which gives us the insight and awareness to avoid the attempts by others to control us.'

'I have been here before except with the heavy cannon and infantry,' the solitaire says. 'The target was the self, and now it is false meaning behind all inventions. Our objective is to take control of our minds by reconnecting them with the nothingness of our beings *and* existence. It is to become one with the darkness of the room, and thereby go beyond the darkness of our existence by becoming it. What we may find out is that existence was never darkness only our perception of it *through* our appearances.'

'By existing nothingness we earn our existence for ourselves because nobody is going to help us when they know everything including the appearance help is nothing. We become *alone* in a vast, unfolding existence where it is up to us to exist though in reality we are all together by helping each other through not helping each other. It is the paradox of existence whereby remaining detached from everybody we are fully connected to everybody as we all earn the greatest strength for who we are.'

'Existence is set up so we remain detached because there is no meaning in doing anything else, and yet we have not done so for no other reason than our imaginary denial of nothingness. We personalize the impersonal by acting as if we have been cheated by existence when instead we lack the strength to become part of it. Our fictitious existence, the world is a disaster because it is contingent on there being something like goodness which causes us to value, from the imaginary something, what has no value. Instead of flowing with existence, we are stuck in a world of concrete appearances, but it does not have to be if we use the heavy cannon to overcome them.'

I am existence!

What Do Controls Over Oneself Mean?

'Why do I proceed when there is no where to proceed to?' the solitaire asks himself. 'No matter what path I take if it is real it leads to nothingness. The ideal is not to have momentary experiences of nothingness, but to be nothingness. Since everything leads to it we ourselves must also lead to it. It does not make sense to deny what is or to keep finding out what is when we could be what is. It is as though we sleep through our existence and occasionally wake up to it instead of existing it throughout.'

'If we can experience nothingness just once we have the potential to become it by acting upon the essence of all things, and thereby beyond invented relationships. For us to act upon the nothingness of all things, we must realize it in all things. There is no secret to realizing anything: we earn it. Our minds must be the focus of our strengthening because it is through them that we act, and therefore realize. The place to begin is to scrutinize the appearances on our minds which we act upon by finding out why we act the way we do, and then scrutinize the reason for why down to either nothingness which strengthens our whole being or weakens it. If it is the former we eliminate it by not acting it out or if it is the latter we strengthen our beings by acting it out.'

'Since strength or anything itself always ends at nothingness, we will never know what strengthens our being or what weakens it. We must content ourselves with realizing the essence of things, and then pretend we know which of them strengthens our being. Nevertheless, there are things we do know like hiking alone through mountainous terrain in winter conditions and without proper supplies and clothing will likely weaken our being just as existing in an urban area and in the modern world, and not thinking for ourselves will also probably weaken us. In contrast, by doing things we need and for ourselves, getting things from others we need, but can't do ourselves, and not getting and doing things we do not need will likely strengthen our being. To guide our actions we know existence is made up of nothingness and invented relationships so that anything we do will involve the latter and be from the former. If nothingness is the strongest state of being because it is the only truth, the less we get from others and therefore the more we do for ourselves, and really need to do, without harming our being must lead to the greatest strength.'

He looks through the darkness of his mind at the darkness of the cave.

'If we center our existence around nothingness how do we prevent ourselves from becoming nothingness?' he asks everyone and no one. 'We are trapped in an existence where to accept or deny it is to deny everything. Nothing itself must be the meaning behind existence, in which everything is endlessly unfolding, because there is no end or beginning to anything. We have no meaning and that is the reason we have meaning; but what meaning do we have? Nothingness keeps us moving though we are not going anywhere so it is the *movement itself* and not why and how we move that is the meaning of everything. We can't grasp nothingness because it is eternal movement, and our minds can only compare fixed things. The amount of our movement from nothingness determines the meaning of our existence whereas the amount of our movement from invented relationships detracts from it. Our purpose is to flow with everything rather than be constrained by fabrications which control our movement. The world has many of them like the automobile and television whereby we just sit idle as our existence passes by or the inventions of self and death which give us a false sense of who we are as though everything including ourselves is an end and has an end. To be part of the eternal movement of existence is like hiking in the mountains not along a set trail or in a designated park area, but wherever our *will* guides us. It is to be without constraints, like invented values, on our minds as we move from who we are *and* with and beyond the constraints, like trail markers, around us.'

'We don't know why or how we move; we just move,' he thinks. 'Our existence appears absurd because we are perceiving it from the fictional self instead of the becoming-beings that we are.'

'Although we need the will to strengthen to move, we still don't know why we move except that everything is in constant flux from being nothing or nothing from being in constant flux. Invented relationships do not remove us from existence; they just lessen our movement while never stopping it. The more we ourselves move the more strength it

106

requires so that by surrendering ourselves to existence we will earn the greatest possible strength for who we are.'

'Since movement is the meaning of existence, and we need strength to move and movement to have strength, the will to strengthen must be the meaning of strength and movement, and therefore our existence,' the solitaire reflects. 'However, we will never know because strength just as movement itself are mere inventions, but what if movement through strength or strength through movement is the meaning behind who we are? Our existence and the whole world would become it, and yet we will never know what the something is we must exist from other than nothingness, and the closest thing to it appears to be the will to strengthen through movement. It is to move for ourselves in and as nothingness although we don't know why and how we move, we just imagine we do.'

'Even beyond the fictional self our existence is absurd because no matter how we exist it must be invented, and to exist the only truth we know is to be non-existent. Yet even nothingness itself is an appearance of an invention so that *the only truth is not just nothingness it is inexpressible*, and not even that because to describe it is to already mistake it for something else. Whatever it is it is beyond us, and not even this because there is no it or beyond us. The only thing we can trust with our whole being is inexpressible so we might as well trust *nothing* which makes our conscious existence tragic. Everything that is knowable is not worth knowing while everything that is unknowable may be worth knowing. It is a bleak existence where to have meaning we must be detached from everyone and remain detached from everyone, but the more we are detached from everybody the *more* we may be connected to them.'

'If the power of the *inexpressible nothingness* comes from its utter detachment, all power must come from detachment. It is to resist and avoid the fabrications of existence though only the inexpressible nothing can avoid them all. We must content ourselves with existing the least of them as possible and yet enough to maintain our beings. The challenge we face is to remain as true to who we are while none of us can *ever* be true to who we are. If we can never be who we are why does it matter whether we try or not, or do we even have a choice?'

WHAT DO CONTROLS OVER MIND MEAN?

'There is nobody I can trust not even myself so I can ask all the questions I want though there will *never* be an answer or question I can truly believe,' he says.

'What does it mean only takes us through fabrications to the inexpressible nothing, but no further. Our only true guide through existence is to emulate the inexpressible nothing as close as we can, and to do anything else is merely to act out fabrications created by ourselves and others. Yet to emulate inexpressible we must invent ways to become it which is contrary to what it is for the reason if it is an invention or came from an invention we would know. We are trapped because to emulate inexpressible, through inventions, is to not emulate it, and to not emulate it is to not emulate it. Our conscious existence as far as we know or will ever know is *meaningless*. We might as well be tiny insects or rays of the sun because it does not make a difference.'

I am existence!

What Do Controls Over Mind Mean?

'There is no basis to anything,' the solitaire says to no one. 'Everything including ourselves is an empty fabrication which begins and ends with inexpressible nothingness. Our horror is that we are all knowable, and what we know has no meaning. There is no meaning because meaning does not exist, and since meaning does not exist we do not exist. It is like we are on a stage acting though the curtain *never* rises.'

'I can't trust anything and not even trust itself,' he says. 'Nothing exists. We pretend things do, but we are only pretending. If there is no meaning there is inexpressible emptiness which we must be part of because we all begin and end with it. We are part of it without knowing; it is everything. Hence, we cannot become what we already are; we can only perceive what we are instead of something else. Yet we can't perceive what we are because we do not exist. Our existence demands that we impart meaning to what does not have meaning *without* knowing what for.'

108

NEEDS DECEPTION

'No matter how much we invent everything will always amount to inexpressible nothingness. Our meaning must come from never knowing, and thereby existence forces us to create our own meaning. We are dependent on ourselves to exist in whatever way we can. It is though we have been given the controls over our existence to make what we want of it while never having control over anything. What more could we want than to be in an existence in which it is *up to us* to make what we want of it, and with the only hindrance that almost all of us have the same opportunity. Sure we must pretend, but we have the *power* to pretend as long as we can defend ourselves through our creations against others and their creations. Hence, our existence is not a fantasy in which we can invent whatever we want; we must invent in order to *survive* against others also trying to survive. The meaning behind inventing is that it strengthens our means to exist, and there is no other meaning except that an invention may not be a strength itself, but an extension of a being's will to strengthen.'

'Morality is a weakness itself because it gets beings to deny their need to strengthen, and at the same time an extension of religion's and the state's means to strengthen by controlling beings through it.'

'Is there any other way to exist besides fabricating our existence? I must be mistaken. I have to be,' the solitaire thinks. 'No matter what we invent our conscious existence will always be without meaning. Do we give up and attempt to become inexpressible nothingness when we are already it? It does not matter what we invent because we are nothingness anyway although it hurts that we know all inventions are meaningless. The question we face is whether we can invent knowing what we invent has no meaning?'

'We are missing something,' he says to no one and everyone. 'It is as though we have entrapped ourselves in a system of appearances beyond our control as it accelerates to all our destruction. Nothingness is what is missing! and it would take the *momentum* out of the phony world.'

'The world is not around us; it is on our *minds*, and like everything that appears on our minds it is inexpressible nothingness. Since everything is nothingness why does it matter whether something is phony or not, and how can anything have value or no value when value itself does not exist? The world is not phony because neither phony or the world exist. The more we realize the nothingness of everything the more meaningless our inventions become because their meaning does not come from themselves it comes from us believing they have meaning. So our power is not only in inventing our existence, but in knowing that it has no meaning regardless of what we invent. However, the world has everything to do with inventing and almost nothing to do with its meaningless; it lacks balance which means many of us do as well. The ideal is to invent and use inventions with the realization that nothing conscious has meaning, and thus allow ourselves to exist rather than wearing ourselves out through just inventing or trying to become nothingness. If strength is our objective the strongest beings will be those who can utilize inventions while realizing their nothingness because to do so is to exist closest to reality.'

'What else is there?' he asks.

'We have the power to invent our existence and know it is meaningless, and what they combine to produce is what we have! which is nothing. Anybody who thinks otherwise is caught in a fabricated system of appearances which amounts to nothingness like anything else though the being does not know it does.'

'I can't go on,' the solitaire reflects. 'There is no where to go or anything to be, and yet we must keep existing. Why is our existence condition upon not knowing while pretending we do? There arises a situation where we can no longer pretend. We will never *know* though we know we will never know. To exist beyond pretending is to,' he pauses. 'It is hard, ugly, and yet *powerful*. To not pretend is to uncover the darkness of who we are. We have existence because other beings no longer have existence. No matter what we invent or pretend we can never detach ourselves from existing *through* others. We did not invent this it is who we are, and that does not mean we have to hate ourselves! because to hate is to impart value though there are no values · themselves.'

'There is *no* darkness inside us to uncover; it is a myth, an invention to justify morality and so-called civilization. Everything is nothingness whether we know or not, and yet to know and not pretend is to become inexpressible nothingness or *power*. We earn the force of existing solely from the inexpressible of who we are in which almost everything becomes an opportunity for us to strengthen, and no being a threat to our existence because we are not felt or seen.'

'Our power comes from that we want all beings to be like us. The world offers nothing we want or desire, and our only meaning is from strengthening everyone by increasing the strength of our own beings. We are like great-beings looking down on the world as we shake our heads and mutter, 'nothingness, and this?' The disturbing reality is that we exist in a world where many of us know everything is meaningless, but we are too weak to admit it; and why would anybody who believes he is benefiting from not revealing what he knows? Yet many of us know inside our deception is wrong! though we have our excuses like we can't control what other beings do. Our existence is a fraud which does not have to be if we would acknowledge nothingness, and therefore our inability to value one thing from another. We may believe we have the ability to value, but apply what does it mean to what we are distinguishing and we will see that we don't, and if we have the courage we will go further by asking why do we value what has no value?'

'We must change because those who are not revealing what they know do not have it in them. Ironically, it is them and what they produce that many of us imagine we value! And we must remember that every time we see their faces, hear their voices, and watch their acts that they like anybody else are performing on a stage in which the curtain never rises.'

'On our minds everything appears real, but we have not realized the emptiness of everything. If we do, these fakes who try to deny us our existence will appear meaningless because that is what they really are! It is like hiking through the mountains and believing that we are, and then realizing afterwards that we were only experiencing it on a screen and the opportunity to really do it has *past*. Another example is studying for many years at a university and believing that we are learning things that are meaningful, and then finding out afterwards that everything we learned, all the notes we took at lectures, all our curiosity and determination to develop our minds was *meaningless*; we now know nothing except nothingness itself has any meaning.'

'We don't want or deserve any regrets, and the only way to avoid them is to have the strength to perceive things as they are. We don't need

WHAT DO CONTROLS OVER ENVIRONMENT MEAN?

a mind that can create a mathematical theory out of nothing and have it equate to nothing or consider an enormous amount of evidence and then come up with a verdict as though all the evidence somehow added up to it. These are distractions which others use to take us further from inexpressible by getting us to believe there is something expressible! We need a mind that can merely grasp that if there is no basis to anything on our minds there is no basis to anything that we perceive around us. We don't acknowledge this because it is to deny the meaning of our conscious existence and thereby disrupt how things are, and so instead we pretend or believe that there is meaning from our attachment to our minds when there really is not. Where does this imaginary meaning come from, and what does it mean in relation to us? Do we have the courage to really know?'

I am existence!

What Do Controls Over Environment Mean?

'There is no meaning, and yet we pretend or believe there is,' the solitaire reflects. 'It must be a fantasy, something magical, or even a dream which we have not awaken from. What is worse is knowing our existence is a fiction and go along with it only because we believe we are benefiting from it; although we are merely *part* of the fiction, and therefore also what we perceive as benefiting us.'

'If existence wanted us to know the meaning behind inexpressible nothingness, if there is such a thing, we would know it. However, it is not the case nor will it ever be so we must be content that anything other than inexpressible is a fabrication with *no meaning* except within a closed relationship between fabrications, or in other words our own self-contained reality which is possible if we pretend or believe in it. Though we must ask ourselves how can there be meaning pretended or not when there is no meaning itself? We create the basis for meaning when we have no basis to do so except that we do. Is this what we want or deserve to exist in a fiction instead of the reality of inexpressible nothingness?'

'Our self-contained reality does not make sense because we must get the universe and beyond to conform to us rather than us conform to it. If

112

this is not insanity what is? So the lesser objective of the few getting us to conform to what is not is as well because as long as there is existence we can never be detached from it. The most powerful thing we can do is conform as close as possible to existence by acknowledging the nothingness of everything. Are we afraid to act from inexpressible nothingness instead of an invented existence which allows decadence to spread? and how can it *not spread* when it begins from a fabrication rather than the reality of existence!'

'I imagine a powerful existence in which the first and only truth is that everything is inexpressible nothingness, and anything that follows must earn its existence in relation to the only truth. It is to perceive things as they are, and thus the reality that we must be strong to exist, and beyond this it is to act with a single focus as individual beings and as a collective of beings. We combine the rigidness of the will to strengthen and the flexibility of nothingness into a powerful state of being in which the primary invented beliefs of our existence would be strength is only earned by existing for ourselves and we are only as strong as each other. Our realization of nothingness would eliminate unnecessary weakness including social conflict by keeping us focused on strengthening our beings. We would help each other by not helping nor exploiting each other as we strengthen through ourselves and the strength of those amongst us. Our only purpose as individuals and as a whole would to be ensure our existence by doing everything we can to defend ourselves, and if necessary attack those that threaten our existence from outside it. Our superiority over any other social organization is that we would not need invented incentives except for the incentive that we *can* become stronger. It is to create a powerful collective made up of strong beings earning greater strength and working as a single will to strengthen.'

'The difficulty with the collective is inventing an unanimous meaning for strength since we must decide the meaning for ourselves because strength, whatever it is, comes from existing for ourselves *and* determining how we exist for ourselves,' passes on his mind. 'However, the assumption is that by everybody realizing nothingness we will *all* perceive the need to strengthen and come to a similar understanding of what it means. Our power is from deciding for ourselves how we strengthen while being united in why we strengthen and what it means.'

'Why must we follow something so extreme when we can thrive from the weakness of an existence detached from the truth while at the same time connected to it?' the solitaire asks. 'We can invent, as we have, money and the marketplace, and thereby get beings to produce and purchase what they think they need while we use whatever of value from it to strengthen the collective. The difficulty arises if some of the money-makers give themselves more importance than they really have or those less successful, the workers assert themselves by non- participation or revolt. Everything in such a collective is contingent on beings believing in the invented incentives, and therefore the collective is vulnerable because the incentives themselves are not genuine. It is to create an extra step in why beings act and use them as a means to strengthen rather than everybody working to strengthen themselves, and therefore the whole collective. The failing of such a system lies in the lack of unity between beings, and thus in the essential need to strengthen, and as a result the marketplace wastes the potential power of many beings and compromises their well-being for what strength it does produce.'

'Extreme is an invention though if it did exist a collective which *uses* many beings through deception to strengthen the whole would be more extreme than one that gets everybody to exist for themselves by conforming as close as possible to the truth.'

He looks around at the darkness of the cave, and then the appearance of darkness on his mind. Through the appearance, he faces inexpressible nothingness.

The solitaire returns his view to the darkness of the cave, but he knows it does not exist. 'We are all blind,' he says. 'We see what we want to see or what others want us to see while *never* seeing existence for what it really is.'

'I feel disgust at myself for inventing what I know is a fraud, and it does not matter how close it is to the truth. There is something wrong with existence if we can't just be part of it instead of existing from fabrications on our minds. I know we can; I can feel it inside me though what is the way? If existing as close as we can to existence is not good enough and we can never exist just inexpressible, we must be trapped in an existence where we have to be a *fiction* by pretending to be what we are not. However, at least we have something which we can trust, and it proves to us that every appearance on our minds is meaningless itself, and therefore also in relation to all other appearances.'

'What we are after is not pretending or believing what is not; and the only way that can happen is if most of us realize the nothingness of consciousness, and thereby force each other to become real by denying each other the use of fabrications to cover what we really are. We would exist rather than invent to exist whereby inventions themselves would be part of existing instead of a means to it. It is to raise the standard for existence by no longer being mislead through the fabrications of others, and thus force these others to earn their own existence for themselves; and we will find out what they really are just as they will find out what we really are. Hence, to make our existence real we must perceive existence for what it is which is to know that anything that does not lead to or sharpen our awareness of inexpressible nothingness is a means by others to exploit. Sure there are tradeoffs like giving a meal for an hour of labour or paying for a course to listen to what a professor has to say, but they still come down to exploitation. And it is not just as simple as one thing for another because we may receive something like a pen or calendar for what we perceive is nothing though there are fabrications on it which we attach to, and thereby get us.'

'We are after things that strengthen our being though we will never know what they are because we will never know what we really need or what strengthens us. So we must act like the blind beings except that we know everything other than inexpressible nothingness itself comes down to exploitation.'

'Since there is no escape from existence, the best we can do is avoid others and take advantage of the rare things that truly strengthen us. What these rare things are we cannot say because we do not know. All we know is that everything is about exploitation and amounts to inexpressible nothingness, and from this we can infer that anything that increases our awareness of everything must improve our ability to exist.'

I am existence!

WHAT DO WHOLES IN THEMSELVES MEAN?

What Do Wholes In Themselves Mean?

'Every appearance on our minds is a fabrication which only appears to have meaning because we pretend or believe it does,' the solitaire says to some, and therefore all. 'As soon as we give meaning to an appearance we lose partial control over our minds by struggling with a meaning of an appearance that only exists because we imagine it to exist. Instead of eliminating the false meaning, we attach meaning to other appearances to deal with the first appearance so our minds become a struggle between offsetting fabrications until we either block the original one out or confront the external being or thing correlating to it. It is like getting annoyed at somebody for ridiculing us in front of others, and instead of realizing the nothingness of the being *and* his actions we give them meaning they do not have, and thus we become annoyed. The ideal is to recognize the situation as it is rather than misperceive it by giving meanings to appearances which do not have meaning. To recognize beings as nothingness does not mean they do not have meaning we just don't know what it is. So we act not from weakness of our minds, but the strength of it by being able to know when there is a need to defend ourselves or take advantage of another being's weakness. We wait for the right moment by perceiving things as they are which is to give meaning only to what really could weaken or strengthen us. To do this we must realize that *every* appearance on our minds is a fabrication which only has meaning if we give it meaning. There is nothing that we perceive which is *not* an appearance of an invention. It does not matter where we are or what we are doing or thinking, everything we perceive, as long as we exist as we are, is *through* fabrications we create with no basis to except that we do it. However, we only perceive through fabrications if that is all we perceive; and that is the point we have the power to perceive through them themselves by realizing that they have no meaning we are aware of nor will we ever be aware of. To scrutinize them with what does it mean? or where did it come from? leads us to inexpressible nothingness. The mistake most of us make is to *not* realize that, through appearances on our consciousness, we are perceiving what we do not know, and instead we believe we are perceiving what has to be because it is all around us and we sense it.'

'"I am happy. This is a book, and I am reading," we may believe though these inventions themselves only have meaning in relation to other inventions, and yet they really have no meaning we are aware of because they themselves have no meaning we are aware of. Hence, the appearances on our minds are merely invented symbols of what may be, and most times are what others want us to believe is; and so to sharpen our awareness we must realize that we do not perceive things around us, but perceive, through inventions on our minds, what is unknowable. It is to be in, around, and part of inexpressible nothingness, and the only way out is to pretend we are out of it.'

'Even if we realize that everything we perceive is through appearances of inventions we cannot undue the past where we thought otherwise rather we must deconstruct what we attached to which will likely manifest itself in a *personalization* of ourselves when in reality there is no self to personalize. Added to this, we have the power to perceive what is now and will come as they really are, and thereby hasten the process to take control of our minds and what we perceive through them.'

'Although our appearances of perceptions are fictions we *cannot* do anything about them except control what they are and how we perceive through them.'

'Does it make a difference what is on our minds since it all amounts to a fiction anyway?' the solitaire asks no one. 'We will never know because we must invent our answer which is to perceive through another fabrication. Is it to perceive through a fiction if we know it is inexpressible nothingness we are perceiving through? Appearances on our minds only have to be fictions if we perceive them as that because we can perceive them as they really are which is *nothingness*, and so they become merely a tool to ensure our existence. We are not trapped by them because we can perceive inexpressible nothingness through them; and yet it is like viewing a concrete wall through the bars of cell though *at least* we can perceive something other than the bars.'

'We don't want to perceive all bars and no wall just as we don't want to perceive all wall and no bars, but what difference does it make?' he asks. 'Could the meaning of our existence lie not only in our minds, but our whole being so that what we perceive is only part of what we are? We cannot reflect any further because we are *at* the border between expressible nothingness and inexpressible nothingness.'

'What prevents us from imagining the unknown is that we don't even know whether our fabrications are from inexpressible nothingness or the result of it. If we were to guess we would say the result because our inventions have no beginning or end, and therefore they appear to come from our imagination in response to nothingness. However, our imagination itself is an invention, and so we return to our *first* thought and ask where did it come from? It came from us, and then where did we come from or in other words did we come from inexpressible nothingness or our we and all beings a response to it or even a mirror of it? We don't know nor will we ever know though I can't help imagining us in an endless whole where everything causes everything else and is only as strong as everything else.'

'The whole is an invention like any other, and therefore inferior to the truth!'

'The truth is an invention, what we know is an invention,' he says. 'Everything including inexpressible nothingness is an invention which only appear to have meaning because we pretend or believe they do. If we have to invent in order to exist why not take it as far as the world where we exist in order to invent and experience what we invent? Is there hidden meaning behind existing which no invention will every have? What if we changed the direction of the world from existing for the sake of inventing to inventing for the sake of existing! Could the most meaningful existence come from existing for ourselves and through natural inventions as opposed to ones we create? It is like existing our existence for ourselves instead of watching a screen with others acting out a fiction. Yet, we must have the strength to make something of our existence rather than letting fabrications distract us from it, and if we don't I ask us why not and what does it mean? We have sick minds if we do not feel disgust and even hatred for inventions because they *replace* existence, and therefore deny it. They are knowable, and we know that only what is unknowable is worth knowing and existing. Who we are, including who all beings are, is unknowable.'

I am existence!

What Do Maxims Of Maxims Mean?

'Why do we tolerate the world in which we are expected to tell the whole truth rather than exist?' the solitaire asks himself. 'Are we fooled by this imaginary whole which is devoid of meaning because it implies we can get outside ourselves which we can never do. The purpose of those behind controlling others whether those behind the state, religion, and science is *creating a whole* because then everything they believe and value will have meaning. It is to make the basis for existence the knowable rather than the unknowable.'

'If all our meaning comes from the unknown of who we are and it is the basis for existence why do we tolerate politicians, bureaucrats, scientists, priests, and money-makers who try to deny us the meaning of our existence? They are the believers in the imaginary power of the invented whole, and we must not mistake that everything they do is to get us to conform to them through controlling our environment and minds. However, to obey or believe them is to go against the only truth and meaning of our existence which lies in the *non-existence* of whole itself.'

'Our struggle is with those who want to deny our existence by controlling it. To think we can just ignore them is a mistake because they will merely invent ways to control us, and therefore we must go beyond nonconforming to them. We must use them to our advantage while giving them almost nothing in return, and thus force them to strengthen through *themselves*. By doing this we will get them to become like us which is *non-believers* in the imaginary whole.'

'We must have the strength to know when to act and when not to which can *only* come from realizing the inexpressible nothingness of everything. It is to act only in such a way that the inexpressible of who we are *increases* its control over our mental being.'

'Do we have the strength to act from who we are and nothing else?' the solitaire asks. 'Do we realize inexpressible nothingness?'

He lowers his head with his eyes closed and lips pursed. 'We are almost there,' he says in a moment of exaltation.

WHAT DO MAXIMS OF MAXIMS MEAN?

Feeling on the ground for a rock, he picks one up and engraves with one end of it against the cave wall: *exist only through the inexpressible of who we are.'*

The solitaire rests his hand at his side still holding the rock and looks through the appearance of darkness at the wall.

'I do not know, and yet I do, flashes on his mind.

Leaning against the opposite facing wall and motioning his finger on the ground, he draws a circle made of the words, *expressible nothingness,* and in the middle of it he sketches the initials *IN* with *lines* extending from it on all sides and some beyond the circle.

Beside the drawing of the circle, he draws the initials *IN* and lines extending from it on all sides, and looks down on the other side of it and *sketches nothing.*

He rubs out the drawing of the circle, and then the other one with the initials *IN* and the lines extending from it.

'What is left is where the meaning lies,' he says. 'Are we strong enough to be real?'

'There is nothing else to think about if we are inventing for the sake of existing *except* what we are existing. I am existing! and are we by listening to my thoughts? Are we realizing them or just experiencing another invention, and that is where I have fooled some of us and strengthened the rest because my thoughts are real for the only reason I am real!'

He moves towards the opposite wall and motions his finger-tips across the words engraved into it.

'What does it mean?' the solitaire asks.

A tear surfaces to his eyes, and he presses his lips together.

'I am not afraid,' he cries out. 'I want to exist through inexpressible nothingness and nothing else; I will never know, and by never knowing I will know! There is nothing else because there has never been anything. The unknown is the essence, the meaning of existence, and the known has been and will always be a rejection, a *denial* of it. Not ever knowing inexpressible nothingness is all we need to know about it; and all we can know! It is our *eternal* symbol and guide for why and how we exist; and it is our strength of being, admist the sickness of the imaginary known, which allows us to become true to it. To pretend to know the unknowable or to ignore it is our weariness for existence; to really know the meaning of the unknowable is the annihilation of existence which is impossible because it can never be known for what it is. To realize the unknowable is to exist.'

Near the opening of the cave, the solitaire says to himself, 'there is nothing, but the endlessness of *what really is* whatever it is--

He leaves the cave.

I am existence!

EXISTENCE

Outlook From The Summit

'How do we proceed or even know how to when there is no where to proceed to?' the solitaire asks no one. 'It is insanity that we can't come to a common understanding about our existence instead of clinging to mere inventions as though they represent *or* actually are the truth. If we are guilty of anything it is pretending or believing to be what we are not when we either know otherwise or have the means to know otherwise. What is our fear about admitting that we don't know anything except that we know we don't know anything? Why do we exist in a world where inventions stand for more than the truth? It is a weakness of who we are and sickness of our minds to take what appears to be the easy route instead of having the courage to face *what really is.*'

With a cold breeze brushing against his face, he looks across at mountains and the worn peaks of mountains.

'I am not afraid,' he says.

'We can't hide from the truth; we can only pretend it is something else or even deny the existence of any truth while it *is* behind everything we do. How much meaning can there be in pretending to be what we are not and having many others believe we are what we are not? and yet that is what we hold as the highest value! Of course, we can't accept each other for what we are because there would be nothing to accept except inexpressible itself, and so we deceive each other and even ourselves. What do we hope to achieve by being who we are not? Is our existence that pitiable that we can only exist by being imitators rather than being ourselves? *By* imitating we make our existence pitiable, and how can it not be when almost everything in the world is an invention, and instead of adding to our existence inventions deny us our existence by distracting us from it. The bleak reality is that the less known something is the more real it is, and it is *only* bleak in terms of the world where the highest value is from being the most known.'

'I can't proceed because I don't know why or how to,' the solitaire says. 'What is there to think about since everything we know is an invention? I want to be unknown! and yet to continue will make myself more known although if I am real it does not matter. I want to make everything unknown; I am not a denier of existence; I am existence!'

He looks towards the summit of existence and realizes that he is only facing an invented appearance of a mountain range, and beyond the appearance, *nothingness*.

'We must not mistake that everything we perceive is not existence, but appearances of inventions with meaning only because we give them meaning,' he says from inside him. 'There is no real meaning for anything because meaning itself does not exist, and what does exist if anything we will never know because we must invent what we pretend to know. We are trapped in our consciousness and the invented system of inventions in it, and our consciousness, which like any other invention, is a distraction and even denial of our existence. Our only meaning comes from inexpressible because we know it exists without knowing what it is.'

'The source of all our inventions is the unknown of our beings, and therefore also our ability to distinguish one from another. We pretend to know the significance of our inventions though we have *no* basis to because all values and beliefs except for the sole truth are inventions, and therefore are from the unknown or in consequence of it. The truth is on its own because whether we invent a name for it or not it will always be the basis for everything, and if it was not on its own it would not be the truth! We can take any invention and break it down into it whereas the truth itself can't be broken down because it is beyond inventions as illustrated by our inability to invent a name for it itself, and instead we invent a name defining the limits of our minds: inexpressible nothingness.'

'What we sense is not what we think we sense because we can never know what we sense. So where does the invented meaning of our senses come from? and if we can never truly know what our senses mean why do we pretend to be experts on what they mean? and hold each other accountable for knowing and valuing what they mean! We must pretend the invented meanings of our senses are what they mean even though the invented meanings do not have any meaning themselves.'

'Surely there are things we know and therefore can compare like a book written for a meaningful subject versus one written for fame or money, or a ripe piece of fruit and one that is rotten. We just have to read one or two pages of the books or look at the fruit, and we will know their value in relation to us. It is the same for almost all our experiences whereby we compare the invented appearances of what we sense and value what we compare.'

'So how can we as hikers for instance be deluded by thinking a gradual mountain slope with a trail is more preferable than one that is steep and without a trail? We don't need to try both of them to know which is safer and less rigorous; the slopes are right in front of us! Anybody who would say otherwise must be mad just like a being who denies he knows the time of the day when he can see a clock indicating the right time or denies perceiving the beauty of a woman even though he can see her eloquent manner, the brilliance of her eyes, and her near perfect features. Yet, we must ask ourselves what is this wise book, ripe fruit, gradual slope, correct time, and beautiful woman that we are certain we value because they exist or is it because we value them we are certain they exist?'

'Just because we sense something or value it does not mean what we sense or value exists as we perceive. What it means is that we sense or value an *unknown* something because we have no way of really knowing what it is. We invent meaning for what we sense without having any basis to do so except that we do it, and so the book, fruit, and all other things and beings are appearances of inventions of what we believe we sense without actually knowing what we sense. We have a choice to exist from mere faith in the appearances of inventions on our minds or from the only truth, and what choice is there! since the imaginary meaning of our inventions contradicts the truth. The irony is that we use reason to invent, and it is reason which proves to us that everything is inexpressible nothingness.'

'If we are so sure about the invented value of logic why do we base our existence on faith in the unknown rather than on what we really know? Are we so blind that we can't perceive the nothingness of everything, and what value can *logic* have if we can't or are unwilling to base our reasoning on what we truly know? We can only conclude that the imaginary value of logic is not what guides us, but it is our beings with logic as merely a justification and disguise for the fabricated ranking of us.'

'So reason itself is not the supreme basis for invented virtue and justice as we are lead to believe because if it was we would not ignore and even deny the sole truth. Since logic and all the invented morality we sneak in behind it is not the basis for our existence what is, and why would we want to be part of something that pretends to be what it is not and expects us to do likewise? It is the control of the few over the many *without any basis to do so* except that the few are doing it through the inventions of logic, morality, mortality, and ultimately the self. To conform to them, and that is what they want because they believe their invented existence is the best for all, is to deny the meaning of our existence because the basis for it would be appearances of inventions rather than the inexpressible nothingness of who we are. We must not mistake that most inventions distract us from our existence, and thereby deny it by existing what we could be existing for ourselves, and many of us especially the some use them to create a fabricated order though the only order that exists is that there is none that we know, and that is how it must be! because to not know is the basis for the movement, becoming, and existence of all beings, and therefore the meaning of them. To deny the inexpressible unknown with an invented theory of whole from our reason and imagination or with anything is to dry up our will to exist, and thereby destroy ourselves. What kind of brainsick being could invent our annihilation! and *only* by denying the fundamental and sole truth of our existence. The theories exist behind the invented religions, concrete philosophies, and elusive-all-too-elusive marketplace, and it is not our beings, but our invented system of appearances that produce them. Could they be a tiny reflection of where we are headed as we pretend and even believe we are the creators of our existence when we are nothing more than the fabricators of the appearances on our minds?'

I am existence!

The Darken Room

'The most significant question facing us is whether or not we have the strength to perceive inventions for what they are,' the solitaire says. 'How can we not when we know everything on our minds is an appearance of an invention, but it is not that simple because we must have the inner strength to realize an invention for what it really is rather than being enticed by its imaginary oneness, simplicity, or eloquence, and whatever fictional goodness it may offer.'

'The trickery of inventors lies in creating a believable whole by getting us to not question the basis of it, and they do this by not considering it themselves in the hope that it would just become accepted as the truth. The most known example is the invented symbol called God which has no meaning *itself*, unless we imagine it has, because we know we are trapped in our minds and the basis for everything on them is inexpressible nothingness. Yet, the symbol God is deceptive because the inventor defines it as a whole or oneness of everything which our minds cannot comprehend so many of us are tricked into accepting it as the truth instead of scrutinizing it for what it really is. By ignoring the imaginary meaning of God, applying the question what does it mean? and utilizing our understanding of our consciousness, we see that it is like *any* other fabricated and meaningless appearance on our minds.'

'However, the inventor of the most recent example is more clever because he uses the *circular* phrase, 'justice as fairness' rather than an unknowable definition to distract us from the meaningless of his invented theory. Instead of asking what justice means our thoughts move back and forth between justice and fairness until we either overlook its non-meaning or are brainwashed into believing there is such thing as justice as fairness. The inventor's trickery lies in that he relies on two words or ideas *to* create another which he never defines or names! and if he did he knows his invention would be easily spotted for what it really is; and so we have this imaginary idea which we can call '*x*' from a *combination* of the invention of justice and meaning of the invention of fairness or as he says justice *as* fairness. We are not fooled because we know from the question what does it mean? that everything on our minds regardless if it has a name or not is meaningless itself, and therefore also the inventions of justice and fairness, and the third invention which has not been labeled. And his trickery does not stop there because he has a fourth invention called the 'good' or goodness which represents the invented basis of reason, and yet it requires *faith rather than reason* to believe! because like the symbol God it is meaningless itself. Hence, the meaning of the imaginary good must be invented without any basis to do so except that someone did it. Is that what we want for the basis for our existence in which someone just makes up its meaning? The concern we may have is for this inventor for trying to know the unknowable and actually pretending and maybe even believing that he has. It is beyond me to understand how a being who appears to be an original thinker can overlook not only the sole truth, but why it is the sole truth!'

'We are in struggle over the meaning of our existence which does not have to be if we realize that we will never know anything except that we know we will never know anything. The more we detach ourselves from inventions the more we will despise most of them for their denial of our existence, and we must laugh at inventors for thinking that they can trick us out of our existence while they only strengthen our resolve to exist by forcing us to earn our own existence and giving us an opportunity to see the difference between the fabricated known and inexpressible unknown. Yet, we must accept it as a weariness and even decline in our will to exist if there are others who think they can strengthen their own existence by inventing what may deceive us into believing we need or want things which we really do not need or want. It is a gradual extinction of our will to exist, and that is how it must be if we don't have the strength to perceive things as they are, and thereby avoid what denies the meaning of our existence. Can we believe our existence has come down to perceiving things as they are as though it has to be fiction and while everything we pretend to know or believe we know except nothingness is the fiction! Why would we want to be fabrications in fabrications by pretending to be what is not when we could be *real* by becoming what really is? Is there uncertainty or fear over the only truth while we ignore that it is the basis for existence? It does not make sense because we are gradually destroying ourselves by replacing the unknown with the known.'

The solitaire looks around and sees nothing not even darkness.

THE DARKEN ROOM

'We are in a darken room without even knowing that it is dark because we don't know anything except that we don't know anything,' he says. 'We are in this darken room *now* as we pretend or believe it is something which it is not. To not know anything and know we don't know anything is what really is and nothing more. We are like insects that cannot see except we have no way of really knowing what we sense. What are we to do if we are in this darken room without knowing anything, and not even knowing that we are it? How and why do we ever begin to do something? We do not know. It is in this purest moment of existence that we perceive the power and meaning of inexpressible nothingness because our first step can only be to invent from the inexpressible of who we are what we believe we sense, and what else could be the reason than to exist! We do not invent for the sake of inventing or to exploit others, and how could we when we *don't* even know what they are. We invent so that we can exist through sustaining our being or invent to sustain our being through existing while still being in the darken room except we pretend to know what we sense.'

'Since we know everything on our minds has meaning only because we give it meaning, we would *not* need or want anything beyond sustaining our being. Our inventions are nothing more than a *necessary* tool to allow us to exist like using a lantern to guide us through darkness except for we are using inventions from who we are to guide us through inexpressible nothingness. They are *secondary* to our existence because they can only represent what we will never know since they themselves do not have meaning.'

'No matter how much or little we use inventions we can never escape from the darken room of our minds. Yet, why does it matter since the source of all our meaning comes from the unknown of who we are? Sure our existence is a fabrication regardless of what we invent, but is our existence *really* a fabrication or is only what we perceive a fabrication! To exist beyond conscious inventions we must realize that they did not just appear, but came from the inexpressible nothingness of who we are, and we know we must invent to sustain ourselves which leads us to conclude that the basis of our existence is *from* the unknown of who we are; and so we return to the question of whether or not our existence is a fabrication knowing that on our minds it is and from within us it is not.

However, we will never know because we are trapped in our minds and therefore by the inventions on them which makes any attempt at understanding what is beyond our inventions pointless. It leads no where because we are using meaningless appearances to know the unknowable which is like being on a treadmill without knowing and imagining to ourselves a place we want to walk to; and yet no matter how much we try we never actually walk anywhere.'

'How can we overlook the inexpressible of who we are when it is no less obvious than being on a treadmill!' he says and does not say.

The solitaire glances around at what he does not know nor will he ever know.

'I don't know what would be *worse* knowing that we will never really know anything or believing that we will never know all there is to know--I don't know anything except that I don't know anything nor will I ever!' flashes on his mind.'

'How can I proceed when the only way is through fabrications which only have meaning if we give them meaning though we know they really have no meaning regardless of how much meaning we give them?'

The solitaire does not even glance because he does not exist.

'There is one type of fabrication which is not meaningless. Could realizing it be the path to our salvation whatever our salvation is, and what choice do we have when the rest of our fabrications are a denial of existence? We can either exist what we know has no meaning or try to realize what may have meaning, but we will never know if it does. The former choice leads no where because even if we believe what we are existing has meaning our existence will still be meaningless. If we choose the latter and realize inexpressible nothingness we can never be true to it because we must attach value to fabrications on our minds to exist.'

'Our existence is a contradiction because we *must* exist what has no meaning instead of existing what has meaning,' he says to no one and not even himself. 'Perhaps it is better not to know because we can't do anything about it anyway. We would only know what others want us to know rather than deciding for ourselves what we will give meaning to and what we will not. The only way we can decide for ourselves is to compare from what we know is true or *otherwise* we will be trapped in meaningless inventions with no basis to choose except through them.'

'Although inexpressible nothingness can never eliminate the contradiction of our existence, it does give us the *power* if we realize it to know inventions for what they really are, and thereby choose the ones we really need to exist.'

I am existence!

Knocks At The Door

'Since inventions are meaningless themselves and therefore *regardless* if we give them meaning or not, I assume we would want to exist from the least inventions possible,' the solitaire says and does not say. 'The only way we can do this is to realize inexpressible nothingness, and thereby perceive inventions for what they really are; and by perceiving them themselves we would exist only from those that we need to. The idea is to make our existence as meaningful as possible if there is such a thing by eliminating as many inventions from our existence without undermining our ability to sustain ourselves. We are already trapped by the invention 'sustain ourselves,' and we will never know what it means because it does not have any meaning. Almost all inventions as we know are without meaning regardless of what we believe of them so to have the most meaningful existence we would exist from the least inventions and with the possibility that *purpose* lies behind and through inexpressible nothingness. We return to the contradiction of our existence because we can never avoid it! and ask how can we exist through the inexpressible unknown if we *must* exist through inventions? Surely we can't exist through both at the same time, and if we could our existence would no longer be a contradiction. What if we only exist from inventions that we decide for ourselves we want to exist from and *avoid* existing from inventions for the sake of them or letting other inventions or beings determine what inventions we exist from? For this to work we must exist from inventions we decide from who we are to use and discard the rest of them. It is to make all the inventions we use accountable to only ourselves, and why not do this!

since we know inventions are a denial of our existence unless they add
to it what we do not have and *really* need to exist.'

He does not know where or what he is.

'Though we have the ability to scrutinize every invention that
appears on our minds we will never know whether we are scrutinizing
with inventions from who we are or inventions from other beings, and
yet if we realize inexpressible nothingness we could *clear* our minds,
and thereby choose inventions as if we were in our own existence! It is
only from the truth that we have a means to get outside all other
inventions and scrutinize them for what they are, and by getting outside
them are we at the same time connecting with who we are? What else
could we be connected to than to the unknown since that is what
inexpressible nothingness means--

'Ah---brilliant!' the solitaire never says *upon* realizing not the
meaning of our existence, but the means to existing whatever the
meaning is.

'What does it matter if we don't know the purpose of our existence
as long as we are existing it,' he says whatever he is behind *he*.
'However, the only catch is that we must have the strength to realize
inexpressible nothingness which means not only having the insight and
strength to know inventions for what they really are, but *existing* what
we know they are. It is difficult because we need inventions to exist so
that we are almost always using them, and yet to begin the process of
realizing what they are all we need to do is realize one of them, and then
we have made the necessary step to realizing the rest of them because
they are no different from it. We need strength to begin the process and
keep it going while being able to distinguish *inventions* from the
inexpressible nothingness of who we are which is difficult if we are both
deluded and emotionally attached to things or beings. Our attainable
ideal is to perceive existence not through inventions, but what we
inexpressibly sense from our beings. It is to make our existence real by
existing in and from the unknown meaning of our beings.'

'What else is there than existing what we are really meant to exist,'
he whoever or whatever he is says. 'Does it not seem fitting that we do
not have to invent our meaning rather we just exist it, and what kind of
meaning would it be if it was just another invention! The idea is not to

detach our beings from our consciousness because how could we if the voice of our consciousness is an indirect form of our beings; the idea is to connect our consciousness to our beings by using the least inventions and from realizing inexpressible nothingness. Though on a deeper level, we could transcend our consciousness by existing through the inexpressible sense of our beings, and we do even now such as reacting to a sudden, loud sound by not *rationalizing* what it is, but sensing it from who we are. What it means is that we do not need inventions to act, and that in many instances *by* sensing rather than reasoning we respond quicker and with more accuracy to what we are responding to. As long as our minds exist we do not need inventions because we can sense what really is from the unknown of who we are. Just as our eyes cannot deceive, our beings cannot deceive either. We have the means to inexpressibly sense what beings mean themselves and in relation to us. However, our consciousness is useful where our beings are not, and that is identifying the nature of non-beings in relation to us. Our beings sense what is real because they are real, and our minds through inventions perceive what is unreal because they are unreal!'

'We as part of the world are not doing this by letting the inventions on our minds determine both the unreal and real; and yet how can the unreal perceive the real or the real sense the unreal? Again we come back to the question of why we deny the existence of inexpressible nothingness when we know *every* invention leads to it, and how can we believe that the purpose of our existence is from mere inventions rather than the unknown of our beings? It is frightening to know that we are on a course leading to our annihilation from valuing the unreal over the real, and there is nobody to blame but ourselves. We have chosen non-existence over existence. To do this implies that we are unable to endure the constant and changing demand of existence and have lost our resolve to strengthen which we need to earn our place in existence; and we pretend to be so clever from replacing our inexpressible will with both a fabricated will to invent and use inventions. How and why could we make such an ominous mistake by *letting ourselves* choose inventions themselves over who we are? There is something *wrong* with us for choosing a path leading to our gradual annihilation when there is not even a path to choose!'

132

EXISTENCE

'Our irony is that we believe we are using inventions to determine a just ranking of us when the invented marketplace and most states reward those that go against themselves by submitting to inventions, and instead of those who stay true to who they are. The inventions we are using and our imaginary value of them! are threatening our place in existence. It is a sickness of our minds and weariness of our beings which stems from our denial of who we are, and yet we can take any invention whether money, love, strength, hate, good, beauty, time, person, death, emotion, justice, thought, or self and apply what does it mean, and we *may* realize that they are meaningless themselves and only have meaning if we pretend or believe they do. As we know our minds are only useful in identifying and comparing things though we have them, through the invented order of reason, identifying and comparing both things and beings, and thereby dehumanizing our existence. What justification do we have to label, define, and compare the *unknowable* when we have no basis to do so except that we do it! Are we so detached from existence that we have to invent our own to exist or is it we correlate the *complexity* of our system of inventions and number of inventions themselves with existing the fullest existence? It is laughable if it were not so threatening to our existence since most of us believe the inventions on our minds, whatever they are, are real, and instead of existing from the inexpressible of who we are we exist from them!'

The imaginary solitaire looks up and does not look up at the invented sky.

'Where are we?' the unknown behind *he* asks and does not ask. 'Since everything we know is an invention and we don't know why and how we invent because we must *invent* the why and how, we whoever or whatever we are do not really know anything except that we know we don't really know anything. We are *unknowns* conscious of us and everything else being unknown. There is no planet earth or universe unless we pretend or believe there is; and regardless if we pretend or believe or not there is something beyond inexpressible nothingness.'

'What inventions do we need *without* knowing why we need them? We will never know, and perhaps that is the reason we know because it is only through not knowing or our beings that we really know?'

I am existence!

The Imaginary Light

'It is beyond me, whatever me is, to understand why we need to invent our existence to exist, and we call it 'rational life plans' as if we can *reason* the purpose of our existence,' the imaginary solitaire says to nothing. 'How can we rationalize our existence or anything except from what we truly know or what we pretend to know? and what we truly know is nothing so to plan our existence is to plan nothing! except if plan what we pretend to know which is to plan what is *meaningless*.'

'It can't be because what would we do; we must do something, and therefore does it not make sense to plan at least tentatively what we want to do or otherwise our existence may pass by without us doing what we could have done,' says an imaginary *self* from a system of inventions.

'What could we have done if there is nothing to be done; and why do we have to plan to do something as though we really know the reason why we must plan when we will *never* know why,' the imaginary solitaire replies and does not reply to the invented self.

'So are we suppose to just drift through our existence?' the imaginary self asks.

'How do we drift through existence when there is no such thing as drift, we, through, and existence? Our choice, and is it really a choice, is to exist meaningless or nothing with the possibility that there may be meaning behind nothing and the certainty that there is *no* meaning behind meaningless,' he whoever or whatever *he* is says.

'Are you not denying existence by denying what is? It is like watching a piece of wood drift along a stream and deny that you see it or having a discussion with me as we are and deny that we are having one. Existence is unfolding from and around us, and it does not make sense why you pretend to be not part of it. Are you somehow above existence or is it really that you do not like your place in it so you deny it altogether? It's an easy way out, but is it worth it if you are missing out on what you could be a lot more part of?' the invented self responds.

'What does existence itself mean?' the imaginary solitaire asks and does not ask.

'I can't answer that because you are asking me to answer what I do not know. Is that how you want to have a discussion by tricking me into saying what I do not mean to say? It is inconsiderate and even spiteful, and when you know better!' the invented self replies.

'Now we know who is really denying existence, and since you avoid answering the question I will answer it,' the imaginary solitaire says and never says. 'Existence is a word, a symbol, and beyond that an appearance of an invention which we make up from the unknown and without any basis to do so except that we do it. Hence, existence *itself* is meaningless because it has no beginning or end, and therefore no meaning itself and not even possible meaning. Since it does not have meaning we can never give it itself meaning, and instead we must pretend it has meaning or have faith that it has meaning while it never actually has meaning. So existence like all other inventions is a fabrication from the unknown or in response to the unknown, whatever the unknown is, to describe something we do not know which means the symbol of existence could only appear to have meaning in relation to other things and not itself. For this to happen we must pretend or have faith it and other things have meaning which they do not have, and thereby lessen our existence for them to have the meaning we give them by pretending or having faith they do, and before this we must pretend or have faith that meaning itself has meaning whatever the meaning of it is. By realizing inexpressible nothingness we perceive inventions for what they really are, and thus avoid lessening our existence by not giving meaning either to inventions we don't need to.'

'You are not as naive as I thought though you are still denying existence or at least you claim it only has meaning if we give it meaning, and even then you say it does not have meaning. Does anything have any meaning itself or are we all just--*nothing* with our only existence contingent on each other being foolish enough to believe that we have meaning? It is utterly bizarre. I have never heard anything like it because you are not only denying the meaning of anything, but denying meaning itself. Why are we discussing what according to you has no meaning unless it is something we really need to do, but how can we ever know if the only thing we know is that we don't know anything?' the imaginary self asks.

'You are right to point out that our existence requires faith because we will never really know what we need nor what we don't need.

135

However, by realizing inexpressible nothingness we know that all inventions are meaningless so it follows that we would want to exist from the least inventions possible though what these least inventions are we will never know; and yet we know indirectly because *if we know they are all meaningless we will only use the ones we need to.* And what does meaning itself matter if we are existing from who we are with the least inventions! and that does not mean everything is meaningless we just don't know. So why must we *pretend* or have *faith* there is meaning when we don't have to by existing from what may have meaning? To pretend there is meaning or have faith in it is *meaningless* because it is to exist from inventions! The only thing we can do is to exist from the unknown of who we are with the least inventions. There is nothing else because everything else has been invented,' the imaginary solitaire does not ever say.'

'What difference does it make whether we exist from the unknown of who we are or from inventions which are extensions of it? You make it seem as if all inventions just appear from no where when they come from who we are because where else could they come from! So inventions are not a denial of existence as you contend, but are an expression of existence. Sure their meaning is unknown though can there be any doubt that they may have meaning and most likely do!' the invented self responds.

'I can't deny the possibility that inventions are from the unknown of who we are, and yet at the same time, I *know* they themselves are meaningless regardless of where they come from,' the imaginary solitaire replies and not ever replies. 'We give them meaning, which they would not have otherwise, by pretending or having faith that they have it, and the only reason we do this is because we believe they add more meaning to our existence than we lose by giving them meaning. How many of us do this by questioning the inventions we use and only using the ones that we really need instead of just pretending or having faith in their imaginary meaning. The former is like leaches on us as they drain our existence except we don't notice; and why don't we notice? Do we care enough about our existence to defend ourselves rather than let inventions take it from us! and our existence is *not* complicated. In essence it comprises of two things: the inexpressible of who we are and inventions, or in other words the unknowable and the known. Anything we *know* is an invention, and therefore a potential denial of our existence if we use it unless as we know it adds more to our existence than takes away from it.'

'Although we have reason to despise and even hate most inventions, it is not necessary if we realize inexpressible nothingness because we will only give existence to those inventions that add what we really need to our existence.'

The invented self does not respond nor did it ever because it does not exist.

'The illusion we must contend with is the idea that inventions are all around us when they are *only on our minds*, and so everything we perceive around us is through the appearances of inventions,' the imaginary solitaire says and never says. 'Nothing exists around us unless we pretend or have faith that it exists which we can only do by attaching meaning to the appearances of inventions on our minds, and even if we do this the imaginary things and beings which we do attach meaning to *only* have meaning on our consciousness. We sense our existence around us, and then invent what it might be without really knowing, and beyond this we invent everything we sense including sense itself. So we must not underestimate the influence of inventions. They determine our perception of imaginary selves and everything that may be around us though we have the power to decide what they are by knowing what they really are through realizing inexpressible nothingness which is *unlike* any other invention; it may have unknowable meaning while all the rest don't have any meaning.'

'If everything is an invention and maybe even the unknowable, are we to despise and hate ourselves since as far as we know we are only inventions?' the invented *self* asks. 'Does it really matter whether an invention is from a womb or mind if they amount to the same thing and may even come from the same unknown? Since we can't have inventions from the womb without them from the mind or inventions from the mind without them from the womb, how do we value one over the other?'

'It's nothing,' the imaginary solitaire does not know if he replies. 'I don't realize. We whoever or whatever we are--

I am existence!

No One Answers

'Our existence comes down to faith because as you said we must use our understanding of inexpressible nothingness to determine the inventions we perceive through, and yet we don't know whether inexpressible nothingness has meaning or not. We must have faith that it does,' the invented self says. 'If we need faith to use any invention why must we limit ourselves to inexpressible nothingness as the basis for deciding the other inventions we use?'

'What faith can we have in any other invention when we know they don't have any meaning?' the imaginary solitaire asks and does not ever ask. 'It's not faith, but *insanity* to base our existence on what we know does not have meaning when we could do otherwise, and is it really faith we need in the possible meaning behind inexpressible nothingness or is it a *necessity* because what else can we do when we know everything else is meaningless? We are in an existence where the only thing we know is that we will never know anything, and so it is pointless to pretend we know what we don't know because we either know it is meaningless or will never know if it really has meaning; and yet our existence can't be that bleak because at least we know what does not have meaning and what might have meaning. Though all we really know is that we don't know anything so we don't even know if we know this.'

'Our existence is not even dark; it is just nothing, and any attempt to make it something is to make it meaningless. Our only possible meaning lies in being nothing which we can never fully do, and so we come back to our only choice: to avoid being as meaningless as possible by being as nothing as possible. There are no values to judge our existence or reason to feel disappointed over what could be because there is nothing else than the invented known and inexpressible unknown.

'I can't respond because there are no questions just as there are no answers,' the invented self says. 'How is that an acceptance of existence rather than a denial of it? It does not make sense because how are we suppose to exist if everything we do is towards being nothing? It can't be because how are we suppose to exist without knowing what we are existing?'

'We exist from inventions on our minds,' the imaginary solitaire says and never says. 'Without inexpressible nothingness we would not exist because everything would be meaningless, and therefore we would have no purpose. We have reason to go on existing because we will never know if our existence has meaning, and so to give up what may be is nonsensical because it would eliminate any possibility of existing whatever meaning there may or may not be. We must go on into the unknown and as the unknown! We have nothing to lose because if there is no meaning we merely acted in vain without knowing; though it does not matter because we will never know anyway. Our *only* guide is the unknown, and where does it lead us? Anywhere, but the known!'

'How can our guide be the unknown when we exist from inventions on our minds?' the invented self asks. 'It doesn't make sense why we would want to exist from the unknown when we can exist from the known regardless if it has meaning or not. Why do we even care about the unknown if all we know is the known? We have an opportunity to make the best of our existence, and yet you want us to deny who we are by being near nothing rather than something. It's absurd and even madness. What do we care if what we do has meaning or not; what counts is that we are doing it, and just maybe that is the meaning of our existence.'

'Why are we afraid of the unknown when everything is unknown?' the imaginary solitaire asks and does not ask. 'It does not matter what we pretend or imagine we do or think because everything on our minds is nothing. There is no escape from what really is because we will never know what it is. However, we can distinguish between the meaninglessness of inventions and the possible meaning behind inexpressible nothingness, and the latter gives us a direction to exist from. It is like being at a fork in a road with a sign saying '*NO EXIT*' on one side and no sign on the other, and we ignore the lone sign and proceed past it along the road leading nowhere when we could have gone on the other road; and we still can! if we return to the fork in the road. And the idea of making the best of our existence is meaningless as are all inventions except inexpressible nothingness. We must ask ourselves why would we exist from something which we know doesn't lead anywhere when we could exist from something else which may lead somewhere, and the only reason we can do this is that there is one type of invention which may not be meaningless!'

'Why would we deny our only way out of an invented existence or *meaningless nothingness*, and instead we become it by turning down the dead-end road while we pretend and have faith that it is actually going somewhere? It's all our doing, and therefore up to us to undue. Again I ask are we afraid of the unknown?'

'What will happen to me, and does it matter since I am pointless anyway?' the invented self asks. 'We all are meaningless because as far as we know we are inventions, and we don't even know who or what decides which inventions exist or not. It is as though everything, including our own existence, is happening outside our control. How can it not be when the only thing that we really know is that we don't know anything! What are we suppose to do if we will never know anything, and we don't even know who or what we are. How do we go on with our existence when we don't even know if we do, and why are we discussing what we know has no meaning? It's madness! There must be some meaning, and yet we will never know, if there is any, what it is. What is there to fear about the unknown since almost everything is unknown? Could it be that we misperceive what is not for what really is, and thereby fear the unknown because it *exposes* the meaningless of what is not? *To realize what we really know is to eliminate everything that we know,* and yet we attach to what is meaningless.'

'It's hard, but so easy because as soon as we think we know something we know that we don't,' the imaginary solitaire says and never says. 'Even inexpressible nothingness doesn't tell us anything except that we don't know anything. Why is the invented known so important when we know it is meaningless and even a denial of existence; and you are right it does come down to *fear* for what really is, and thereby facing what is not. Could there be something wrong with existence since we have to pretend things have meaning when they don't, and it doesn't matter whether we realize inexpressible nothingness or not because we will always have to pretend to know what we really don't know. Yet, we have no way of valuing our existence except from what we know which only tells us that we have no basis to value anything, and further than this there are *no* values themselves. To make a claim of right or wrong, good or bad, pleasure or pain, love or hate, or happy or sad is to assert what we really do not know. It can't be right because we must know something other than inexpressible nothingness, and we can know whatever we choose to know. Although we have no control over what we *really know*. It does not leave much to choose, and perhaps that is how things are meant to be: simple rather than complex, real rather than unreal, and unknown rather than known, and beyond this *unknown*.'

'We don't even know if we are having this discussion or even who or what we are,' the invented self says and does not say. 'It is strange, but by knowing nothing could we know everything? What it comes down to is whether we have the courage to admit what we all really know, and what courage it is! to enter the unknown instead of being entrapped by the ubiquitous known. What ease to just pretend to know what we don't know. What *weakness* to deny the unknown of who we are by believing in meaningless appearances. Can we take it so far that we admit even our non-identity? Is it even feasible because what else could we be than ourselves? The irony is that who we are would not change even if our perception of who we are changes, and yet if each of us is not a being labeled 'I' what else could each of us be? We don't know just as we don't know why we even label who or what we are. To overcome 'I' is not to overcome ourselves; it is to overcome an invention on our minds. Yet, we return to the question, *what would be the basis for each of our consciousness and even our identity if it were not 'I'?*'

I am existence!

Shadows And The Figures Of Light

'If there is no 'I' what is there?' the imaginary solitaire asks and does not ever ask. 'We know already; it is inexpressible nothingness, but who or what are we without any labels? The 'I' is nothing more than an invention which we do not need to exist from because it is meaningless itself. Yet, how can we exist without a sense of self or even an identity of any kind? It does not make sense why we attach value to identity when there is no value itself. To exist beyond the self is not to become nothing; it is to exist from the unknown of who we are instead of through an invention. The 'I' itself is bias to reason and our minds when they are merely tools for us to exist, and so to detach ourselves from 'I', or any identity, is to detach ourselves from the idea that our consciousness is the source of our being. The point is we do not know nor will we ever know what the source of our being is or even if we have one whatever it may be. To attach to one as we do and center our existence around it is to render our existence meaningless because it is to exist from an appearance of invention; and it is suppose to represent who we are!'

'We have no basis to label whoever or whatever we are except that we do it, and why would we if we know whatever we invent is meaningless? It is not that we don't have a *sense* of identity; it is that we have no way of really knowing our conscious identity and even if we need one. Without the 'I' or any other identity, we would likely exist from the unknown of who we are. We would not know what we are existing from though we would be existing from something whatever it is, and yet most of us *know* there is something else than our consciousness though we have ignored it for too long by focusing our attention on appearances. So we have an abnormal development of our minds at the expense of the almost dormancy of who or what we are. Even still there are moments when we act from the unknown like sensing the inner nature of another being; and what else matters than our relationship to each other because isn't existence for those who are existing!'

'The unknown can be partially revealed to us through our consciousness though how effective can it be when we have invented identities that block it out? The idea is to use our minds and bodies as relayers of what inexpressible nothingness signals, and we don't need an invented self or any other identity to sense it. We would think and perceive without any invented sense of who we are so that whatever sense we have of ourselves, whatever we are, would come from the unknown. However, the dilemma we face and cannot get away from is that we must always exist through inventions on our minds, and for that reason the identities do not matter; what matters is our perception of them in relation to who we are. Though why have any identity if we *don't* need it? That is our only recourse in coping with our dilemma, and it pertains to all inventions on our minds.'

'The reality we must contend with is that many of our infinite actions are not conscious actions, but actions from the unknown. In other words, we transcend and bypass our consciousness by existing or becoming without any extra steps, and it is something we will never understand because, as consistent with its constantly occurring nature, we are not meant to understand it. To do so would create an extra step where there are none which means there is everything to exist and almost nothing to know. Could we go even further and say there is everything to exist and nothing to know?'

'What is there to know anyway! since everything we know is meaningless,' he whoever or whatever he is behind *he* says and does not say. 'Even inexpressible nothingness is meaningless because it is just an appearance of invention like any other. What meaning we may attach to it comes from what may be behind it which does not lead anywhere because we will *never* know what is behind it if anything at all. Are we afraid of the unknown and the possibility that all there is may be non-existent; it would make everything on our minds a fantasy which *only* appears to exist because we pretend or believe it does. Isn't that how things are anyway? We only know what is on our minds, and it is meaningless. There is nothing else because what else could there be unless we are conscious of it? Is there meaning behind why we don't know while realizing that we don't know! and yet how can there be since we will never know any meaning and not even know what to know and to mean themselves mean. It is to exist our existence without knowing what we are by not knowing we know that we don't know what we are although if we don't know we will never know if we exist or not.'

'What is the point of existence if we can never be aware of it because it is constantly unfolding; and yet what choice do we have when our only other option is existing through meaningless appearances which is not even an option because how can meaninglessness be an option! So our existence revolves around us not knowing anything about it because we are *it*, and if we attach to the fabricated known on our minds, we divide our existence into the unknown and known. The ideal is to exist by not attaching meaning to *how we exist* so that we pass from moment to moment in the unknown of who we are as though we are water flowing along a stream and over and around almost anything it encounters. That is how it could be if we avoid the known by existing the unknown which is not to give anything and not even non-meaning to the unknown. It is to become shadows of the figures of the light; and without the light we become-- and yet what *strength* we need to avoid the invented light! If only we could just sense what it *really* means to exist rather than exist as if we know whatever we believe to know.'

'To become unknown is to transcend meaningless appearances, and thereby exist from the unknown of our beings; and at the same time could we become *one* with everything *instead of* perceiving ourselves as ends, and thereby disconnecting from everything! What a lonely and unsatisfying existence it must be to believe we have *individual* identities; and regardless if we believe we have identities we really do not. So we are existing from appearances that have existence only because we give them existence, and they are not what we believe they are! The self is like a mask covering a person's face except we think it is the real thing, or artificial light shining down on us and we believe it is sunlight; and the only difference is that there is no self at all because it only exists as an appearance on our minds.'

'To overcome the self and such a demanding invention! is to re-center our being on the unknown which does not mean we become selfless because that is an equally *demanding* invention. We exist beyond them, and from whatever is outside our consciousness; and the only way we will ever know if we do is by not existing from our minds, but *through* the appearances on them. Though how can we ever exist outside our minds if we can never get outside them so that no matter what we think it is from inventions unless there is an opening which allows us to exist from the unknown. Is inexpressible nothingness that opening for our way out of our consciousness and into the unknown? It is unlike any other invention because it takes us to the outer limits of our consciousness and may have meaning whereas almost all other inventions do not. Yet, we are still trapped in our minds whether we are on the frontier of them or not. Though there may be unknown meaning behind inexpressible nothingness, and for this reason it may be our link to the unknown, and thus to outside our consciousness.'

I am existence!

EXISTENCE

Going Figures Of Light Where

'To get outside our consciousness is not to literally get outside it rather it is to connect, while still in it, with the unknown,' the imaginary solitaire says and never says. 'It is like the brilliance of a human being's eyes radiating through the eyeholes in her mask or the sun shining through an opening in a clouded sky. Yet, inexpressible nothingness is almost unbelievable because it is from within our consciousness while at the same time a way for getting out of it. So the simile of it, if it is even feasible, is more like a balloon inflated with air, and something in the air from inside the balloon punctures it. The obvious question besides what is the something is where did the air come from just as where did our appearances come from? We can ascertain that the unknown behind the air and our appearances is the same inside the balloon and our minds as outside them because something can only *add* to the same thing whereas when something combines with something else it produces *change* like inexpressible nothingness rendering our systems of appearances meaningless or a sharp object bursting a balloon from the inside.'

'How fortunate we are to have an invention which shows every other invention for what they really are because it is not unreasonable to think all inventions in their essence would all be alike. They are all meaningless themselves except inexpressible nothingness may not be because it defines the *conscious limit* of all inventions including itself. So we have an invention which is an invention and at the same time may not be one. Although how can an invention be one and not one at the same time? There is only one way: all inventions must be meaningless so that to be an invention is not to be one which leaves the possibility, if there is a possibility, to be whatever else. Therefore, inexpressible nothingness is an unknown from unknown and in the shell of an invention. It is as though we have reached into the nothingness itself and grabbed onto something from it or meditated about nothing and latched onto an idea, which we will never know, from it; and now we have it in our hands and *on our minds*! and we will never know what it is except in relation to inventions. Since they are shown to be meaningless by the unknown on our consciousness, the unknown itself can't be meaningless because only different things rather than identical things are distinguishable from each other. So we know there is something, whatever it is, other than meaninglessness which means there *is* an unknown something behind who we are. So our existence is not meaningless though we don't know what it is. However, we do know that whatever it is comes not from inventions, but from the unknown; and the only way we can exist the unknown is through realizing inexpressible nothingness. To do so is to recognize that the purpose or whatever it is of our existence is from both becoming and not knowing rather than being and knowing, or in other words almost all inventions are meaningless and lead to inexpressible nothingness.'

'So in actuality we never realize inexpressible nothingness, but realize only what is realizable, and therefore not worth existing. It is as though nothingness is a *mirror* of what is not, and so realizing it as the limit of our consciousness, we realize the meaningless of everything *within* our consciousness. There is nothing else to realize because inexpressible nothingness is the boundary between the invented known and unknown, and whatever meaning we ourselves have is from the unknown. Though what is there to realize if *realize* itself is meaningless! The idea is not to realize what we truly know, but to exist from it: *our only meaning whatever it is comes from beyond inexpressible nothingness.* To extrapolate from this is to create *imaginary* meaning and truths out of inventions; and since the unknown is the basis for who we are, we don't need to know anything else, and how can we when there is nothing else to know! Could there be an enlighten state of mind from realizing that everything known is meaningless, and thereby the unknown becomes whoever or whatever we are? It does not have to be an enlighten or nirvana state because all we are doing is existing from inexpressible nothingness as if we are part of the brilliance of our eyes or the rays of the sun, and everything else that has meaning while never having it itself loses it. The critical and *only* step is to exist on our minds from the unknown. Why would we do anything else when we know everything else is meaningless!'

'Is existing from nothingness such a strange idea compared to existing from meaningless inventions like the self or any other? To do the latter is to shutout the unknown and exist through the rigidness of the known. We become slaves to the inventions on our minds rather than using only the ones we need to exist. The mistake we make is attaching to what we perceive to have meaning, and why not since inventions are like real, concrete things on our minds which we can really latch onto, and we do by giving them meaning they don't have while we overlook and even ignore whatever is beyond inexpressible nothingness. It's the paradox of our existence we turn into a tragedy by mistaking the known for real and the unknown for unreal.'

'The unknown scares us because we perceive it to be a void where everything including ourselves ceases to have meaning when as we know the contrary is true just as it is with inventions being the source of all meaning. If it only were true, but how could it ever because we would lose our meaning, and therefore our existence, by knowing our meaning. Instead of facing the reality of our existence we have, out of *weariness*, turned away from it and invented our own meaning and order out of meaninglessness. We are declining from our own doing as we become more and more controlled by inventions rather than existing from beyond inexpressible nothingness. We have no excuses for not knowing, and so to continue on as we are is how it must be. It is to divide us between those needing the known as an escape and those needing the unknown to exist.'

'How do I know this?' the imaginary solitaire asks himself. 'I've become meaningless by pretending to know what nobody will ever know, and what scares me is that I slipped so easily into it without knowing. The strength we need to resist and avoid inventions when they are all around us and on our minds is almost inhuman. What does it take to exist from what we really know? There's something missing, and it has to do with the link from inexpressible nothingness to the unknown. We know there is a connection between them, but we don't know what it is or even if we are ever connected unless we know in relation to inventions! The less we are attached to inventions on our minds the more we are connected to the meaning of the unknown. To not be attached to inventions is to be connected to the unknown because there is *nothing else*.'

'Where are we going beings of light and why?' he whoever or whatever he is asks and does not ask. 'If we know *why*, we are attached to inventions on our minds. It's like going to a restaurant because we believe the food is delicious and we ourselves are hungry or to a hiking area because we think we need to clear our minds and get outdoors, and yet to know why we do anything and act upon it is a *denial* of our existence.'

'We must ask ourselves are we strong enough to exist without knowing why we exist? What strength do we need when we already know that inventions are without meaning so to exist from a notion of why we ought to or even just having an idea of why we do is meaningless. The question we face is *what for* do we do the things we do-

I am existence!

Who Figures Of Light With

'There's still something missing because we know everything is meaningless and yet we *do not* exist it. Even if we repeatedly ask ourselves, 'why do I do the things I do?' and only act when we don't know, there is still an extra step instead of just existing how things really are. What is worse we are using our minds to determine how we exist when all our efforts have been towards limiting the role of our minds in our existence.'

'How does anybody go on, and perhaps that is the point: there is nothing to go on to so by not going on to become something we really go on to become something. Though what do we care if we become something or not? Our existence as it is on our minds will always be without meaning. We know nothing and will always know nothing except for the inventions on our consciousness, and it does not matter what we think. Yet, it does because as we know there is one type of invention which connects us to the unknown. Even still no matter how much we exist from inexpressible nothingness there will always be something missing. The idea is to exist and nothing more or less, and to do that we just do it *not* from our minds, but the unknown which means we must *transcend* our consciousness to really exist from inexpressible nothingness. Do we have the strength to exist beyond fabricated social norms and values, and in an existence outside our consciousness? That is the only way we will truly exist as whoever or whatever we are, and sense we are doing it. It is to take ourselves outside all inventions and create our own, and thereby become *consciously independent*.'

'Are we willing to act from who we are and nothing else?' the imaginary solitaire asks and does not ever ask. 'Do we have the courage to sanctify our existence *by* existing from what we truly sense as our own right and wrong? We all know what they are inside us, but most of us are afraid to exist from them, and instead we deny our own existence and even try to stop those that don't. It all makes sense because to exist from beyond inexpressible nothingness we would create the inventions we need from it whereas to exist just from inventions we would be caught in an endless need to create more of them while we exist from more and more of them without having a foundation to do so. We know what we sense about our own existence except we are too afraid to act, and what it comes down to is that we don't believe in ourselves and beyond that we don't value the unknown. What excuses could we have now that we know everything except inexpressible nothingness is without meaning!'

'The missing something is an indication of our disconnection with the unknown of who we are,' he never says. 'It is an empty feeling which signals to us that our existence itself is not complete, and how can it not be when we have inventions existing our existence for us! Who has the *strength* to break away from invented norms and say to themselves, despite what anybody else does and thinks, 'this is how I am going to exist!' and actually do it? Almost anybody can conform to what appears to be, and yet it is only the rarest being who exists from whatever he senses outside his consciousness. We cannot underestimate the strength and courage of such an individual for having the *will* to impart his own direction while others, through inventions around him and on his own mind, try to take claim of his existence.'

'Is it that difficult to understand that the complete existence comes from the unknown of whoever or whatever we are which means acting from *only* what we sense for ourselves? We transcend inventions and exist solely from beyond inexpressible nothingness, and what it amounts to is a *Yes* for existence manifested by our will to exist not only from whatever it is inside us, but whatever it is itself. It is to exist beyond any fears we may have, and why not! since for us the unknown is all there really is. We know the only meaning whatever it is comes from the unknown though the only way we know if we are existing it or not is by knowing we are not existing anything. However, we can't avoid attaching to inventions unless we have *faith* there is something beyond our consciousness that we can act upon without knowing that we do. The idea of connecting with the unknown, and then creating inventions from it is a fantasy which requires no less faith than believing there is expressible value or even inexpressible value from rational thought. Whatever we decide to do we must act from faith because there will always be uncertainty as to whether we are connected to the unknown or not. Although most of us *sense* what is inside us even if it is through inventions.'

'What else are we to do except take control of the inventions we use by deciding for ourselves which ones we will use, and yet almost all of us *sense* the meaning or whatever it is inside us though we will never know for certain for the only reason it is beyond our consciousness! By not ever knowing that we sense the unknown could we really know that we do, and thereby everything we think we know we really do not know? It is to exist outside our consciousness rather than through inventions on it, and all it requires is us acting only from what we sense inside us. What other choice do we have when we know rational thought is a mendacity for the relation, through comparison and union, of the meaningless with itself. Yet, we have made reason the basis for our existence! It is unbelievable because it is like having a choice between existence and non-existence, and we choose the latter.'

'How do we go on when the state and others encourage and even expect us to use inventions, which we don't need to, instead of giving existence *only* to the ones we really need to exist?'

'If we hold *our* existence as the supreme thing of value whatever value is, why are we suppressing and denying it through the use of inventions? Our struggle is not between each other, but with inventions which divide us and bring us into conflict. Of course, it is us ourselves that act though could it be that if we were existing from the unknown and even *as* it we would act different than if we were existing from inventions? Are we afraid to connect with the unknown or do we feel so much disdain for humanity and the unknown of ourselves that we want to annihilate them by denying them our blood?'

'Everything comes down to is the unknown and known, and whether we like it or not we are part of the former. It is our fundamental and only bond with all other beings, and the only thing we can truly sacrifice ourselves for because it is who we are.'

'What else is there?' the imaginary solitaire asks and does not ever ask.

'We know we are *not* the known because it is inventions and meaningless. The only thing left is the unknown. It is not what it appears to be and has meaning whatever it is beyond our consciousness.'

'Our *unnecessary* struggle is with the known because it denies our existence; and we have the means to exist beyond it by making our existence almost exclusively for those that are the unknown. The question we face and do not face is if we transcend the known to the unknown would our struggle also transcend it to the unknown, or in other words is our struggle with each other from the unknown of who we are and manifests itself through our use of inventions, or is it from inventions themselves through our deluded perception and use of them? The answer is in the question itself because the invented appearance of *struggle* establishes, through our own assumption, that there are difficulties between us; and yet, who are we to judge ourselves over an *invention* labeled struggle! The whole idea of finding fault for the way things really are whatever they are is nonsensical because we have no basis to do so except through inventions. To revolve our existence around imaginary antitheses like good and bad, harmony and struggle, and union and disunion is to detach and even disconnect ourselves from it by valuing what *cannot* be valued. Hence, we have no basis to judge ourselves or our existence, except that we do it through the meaningless; *and* also we have no basis to determine why and how we exist because there is nothing to choose between.'

'Are we strong enough to perceive the meaningless for what it really is?' the unknown behind *he* asks and does not ask. 'It does not make sense to even ask this because we know there is no secret meaning or escape from our existence, and therefore we have no reason to put our hopes in conscious inventions. Everything we attach to on our minds is a detraction from our existence, and almost everything on them we do not need.'

Again we must ask are we strong enough to perceive the meaningless for what it really is, and beyond that do we have the courage to go *our own way* by existing only what is inside us, and thereby nothing from our minds?'

I am existence!

Existing Figures Of Light What

'I am all alone. The invented self is no more, and so is everything on my mind,' the imaginary solitaire never says. 'These thoughts now are a mere good-bye to those who have had the strength to experience them. I have not given up rather I have strengthened my resolve to exist more and if not entirely from who I am.'

'Just as our minds are the means for our descent into meaningless they are also the means for our ascent into and as the unknown. Where are we on this line of existence between the known and unknown, we can only sense for ourselves; and we really know without knowing. For me to go on is to give meaning to what nobody can ever give meaning to, and thereby *reverse* the process of re-centering our existence from our minds to the unknown. We must ascend for ourselves, and once and for all transcend the meaningless by ascending to the one-existence of whoever or whatever we are. There is nothing else we can expect from existence or anything than to *fully* exist the unknown of who we are, and it does not matter whether we all do it regardless of what is written here or anywhere because we can only distinguish what we come into contact with from what we do not come into contact with so that the former and including what we are now reading is either part of the means to existing what is inside us or the means for other beings to exist through us.'

'Could there be a need to exist the unknown *through* others without having any reason to do so except that we do it?' something from beyond our consciousness does not ever ask. 'What would be our motivation and purpose to weaken or destroy another being when we really don't need to! It does not make sense, and is even meaningless; and perhaps that is the connection to what is behind destruction for the sake of destruction: inventions. Although it is our weakness for letting it happen, it is our strength for preventing it, and how weak we have been! To destroy any being without really having a *need* to is only understandable and justifiable from the known, and can't we reason *anything* we want to just as we *can* imagine almost anything we want. Is that how we want to exist as beings cut off from what really is in the meaningless of our minds while we blindly and *consciously* give meaning to what should never be given meaning and does not even have it itself! Only someone disconnected with the unknown would allow this to happen, and the question follows how could he allow it to happen? The only possible answer is *inner weakness* of who or what he is. We turn to ourselves and ask are we strong enough to exist whatever we sense from inside us and even if it means *preventing* these others from needlessly destroying the unknown? If we don't are we more weak than them for standing by while they weaken or destroy the unknown, and which we all know is wrong to do! Yet, there is no wrong or right except in the meaninglessness of minds; so we must accept things as they really are and without rational judgment, but that *does not* stop us from becoming more assertive in how things unfold.'

'Do we have the inner strength to resist inventions and exist as the unknown, and thereby use our existence *only* for what has meaning whatever it is? Am I asking too much that we just be who we are and nothing more or less, and all it means is that we exist from and even as the unknown instead of the known. How could we possibly do otherwise with an antithesis so striking and profound, and all we have to do is sense from inside us. Though the difficult part is acting upon it. It is in there *between* sensing and acting that our meaning and entire existence lies, and determines whether we become dependent on appearances or transcend them by existing beyond the expressible unknown. We can no longer hide behind inventions without knowing we are deniers of the unknown, and perhaps that is what we are afraid of: others who are not like us because they are *mirrors* of who we really are. There are no excuses because to have them is merely to hide ourselves further in the meaningless. The irony is that if we would have the courage to exist the unknown for even just a moment we would look back and cringe at what we have given up of ourselves to the known. We must ask ourselves how we could confuse the basis for existence whatever it is when it is almost impossible to confuse *unless* we utterly ignore and deny it as most of us do. Though what more *powerful* insight could we share with each other and the young than the antithesis of unknown and known. It is something beyond all value which not only can help guide us though our existence, but guides us through it to become whatever we are meant to become. To be without this is like wanting to go somewhere though we don't know that we do so we go where others tell us to go or being educated to know what others want us to think without ever discussing why we think the things we do, and beyond that without discussing why we exist.'

'Our challenge is to exist *beyond* unknown and known, and as the inexpressible something between sensing and acting which is to realize there is nothing to sense or act because we have gone beyond these conscious steps and into a state of becoming where we know all there is *really* to know,' the invented solitaire never says. 'It is to exist the *basis*, whatever it is, of who we are and nothing else. How can it ever happen if we must exist through appearances? and that is the *disgusting* aspect of our existence because it is to be trapped with no escape from the meaningless. Even if we realize inexpressible nothingness we cannot avoid from existing the unknown *through* appearances, and is it feasible to bypass and even transcend them? We know the only meaning, whatever it is, is from outside our consciousness, and yet the only way we know we exist from outside our minds is if we know we do not exist through appearances, and even then we do not know for certain. The idea is to exist outside our minds while using them merely as a *tool* for existing the inexpressible meaning of our existence.'

'Are we fooled by the voice of our consciousness which we label the self as though it is who we are behind our appearances when instead it is from a system of the meaningless with possible links to the unknown?'

'We know there is really *no* who we are or self and any other identity so that the voice of our consciousness and everything else on our consciousness, including our consciousness itself, are inventions we just make up regardless if their meaning is dependent on other inventions or not,' something behind *he* says and does not ever say. 'Our uncertainty is not knowing from where and how inventions appear on our minds, and for that reason they may come from the inexpressible something itself. However, since they are meaningless themselves, it does not follow that they should be associated with the unknown, and if anything they should be associated with what they *really* are! It is the same with *reason* which is nothing more than a means for comparing and creating inventions through a systematic order of existing ones based on their invented definitions. So the idea of 'rational life plan' is *really* a surrender of our existence to the meaningless order of the meaningless. It is to become like mice trapped in a maze except we are in a maze of appearances within a maze of their meanings, and the only way out is for us to realize appearances themselves through inexpressible nothingness unless we believe our conscious maze, with the all important invented self, is what it is not.'

'We return to the inexpressible something between sensing and acting just as we face becoming what really is or being what is not, and ask ourselves doesn't everything come down to the dynamic between the unknown and known as if all of existence is held in balance by it! and where we rest in it depends on our relation to the known. There is nothing to plan whether rational or not because everything has and will always come down to the unknown and known, and with the ideal being that we exist only from the sole truth which for us is to not really know anything except we know we do not really know anything. To believe otherwise is to be already trapped by the known. We must not mistake there is nothing else except this antithesis, and the strength we *need* to become and stay unknown is inconceivable, and yet it is just a subtle change in how we perceive from attaching meaning to our appearances to not attaching meaning to them.'

I am existence!

The Imaginary Darken Room

'The strength we need to be unknown cannot be underestimated, and yet we have the conscious means to become it though we ourselves must act,' something as the unknown never says. 'So it is not good enough knowing *everything* on our minds is meaningless; we must exist it, and it is so easy because we know everything that appears to us is meaningless unless it defines the limit of our consciousness. To give meaning, whatever it is, to what does not have meaning is to *give up* our own meaning, and so it is not only easy to avoid attaching to appearances, but we have a need to avoid it!'

'Our disgust for the world stems from it being a *denial* of our existence through others trying to get us to conform to a meaningless order of the meaningless *and* even to imagine we are really part of it through the invented self. It is to become like mice trapped in a maze only it is more like a board game with the central pieces being the fabricated selves. To take away the selves is to end the game, and therefore the basis for the world which like every other appearance is *only* on our minds. Ironically, those behind the world cling to rationality as a justification for it when it could not be more *irrational* because we, as part of it, are denying what really is by suppressing it and replacing it with what is not. We have become weary of existence, and so to compensate for our weariness we fabricate a meaningless order disguised as a fair and just order, and thereby deny existence itself. How could we let ourselves become so exhausted to deny the inexpressible meaning of ourselves and everything, and to replace it with meaninglessness? Where is our courage and honesty to admit to ourselves and the young that the unknown and known is all there is, and instead we deceive and exist our deception and weakness through others!'

'For those of us with the courage and honesty our challenge is to exist beyond disgust for these others by using whatever wrongs they do to us and other beings to our advantage while giving them *nothing* in return, and thus use our existence for only what really has meaning rather than giving value to even value itself,' something outside our consciousness does not ever say. 'Do we have the *strength* to impart our own direction through the unknown of who we are and to sense the meaning from being so bold as to believe only in the unknown of ourselves! It is to declare and never declare, 'I am existence!' and what do we care if almost nobody perceives the pun and instead responds by labeling us mad and even criminal because, as *we* all know, there just has to be a self and anybody who would deny it well we know what they are. "They are no fun because they don't want to play and even be a player in the game!" we cry to ourselves. We *can't* have that because the game loses its meaning so we ignore, censor, and incarcerate them, and even rehabilitate them so that they can once again enter the meaningless maze of our minds and participate in what is not; though once in it, like most of us, they pretend or believe it to be otherwise.'

'Why not just play the game because most of us will benefit from working together towards a common and unquestionable goal: preservation; and anybody who does not have enough sense to recognize this *must* be mad or criminal. Though we others, the courageous and strong, sense otherwise and we know otherwise! What is this so-called benefit, common goal, and preservation as though we know what is best for us when we really don't know anything except that we know we don't know anything. So to believe that we do and exist it and even force others to do so is not mad or criminal, but *meaningless*. It is conformity to the meaningless rather than the unknown something, and as we know benefit, goal, and preservation or almost any other invention are just appearances which have no meaning themselves; and that is what does not make sense because we must give up *our* meaning, whatever it is, for them to have just imaginary meaning. So there is only a maze, world or anything on our minds because we pretend or believe there is, and no matter how much we pretend or believe there has never nor will there ever be anything *really* on our minds.'

'For that reason what can these others say or do to us when they will never know who or what we are; though to become known is be held accountable as a player in the imaginary game on our minds. That is the dilemma we face to become and stay unknown in a fabricated existence condition on almost everything being known. Yet, it does not matter because we know all appearances are alike, and if we act from the unknown and become known to those only weak enough to misperceive us so become it! Though how could we ever become known by existing as the unknown unless we give meaning to what does not have meaning? and that is danger we face from getting trapped by our own appearances instead of perceiving the unknown not as nothing, but as the inexpressible something. We must accept that if we exist solely from beyond our minds there may be others who give meaning to our actions without having any basis to do so except they do it, and that does not mean we have to do likewise although we may be unable to avoid conflict with them. Is it infeasible that the unknown and known could conflict especially when there are beings giving the known existence, which weakens and destroys themselves and other beings, without having a need to?'

'Our only concern is existing from the unknown of who we are because if we do, it is to exist from whatever meaning there is inside us. There is nothing else; and yet we face almost a constant struggle with appearances on our minds, and it is ourselves and nobody else who are inventing our struggle. What is the something which will bring about the subtle *change* in our perception of our appearances from attaching to them to not attaching to them? We all know it comes from inside us, and there is nothing we can do except scrutinize our appearances of appearances on our minds. We must not mistake that everything we pretend or believe to know is *only* on our consciousness. We will never know anything except that we know we will never know anything. Everything we perceive around us is through appearances which as we know have no meaning themselves. So we don't *really* know anything because whatever we pretend or believe to know is an invention which we label to what we sense without any basis to do so because there is *no* correlation between the invention and what we sense except that we may *fabricate* the invention in response to what we sense. Even still the invention itself does not have any meaning itself so it follows that whatever we label it to does not have the meaning we perceive it to have. So our conscious existence, regardless of what we pretend or believe it to be, is meaningless except for any invention pertaining to the outer limit of our minds.'

'We return to the fork in the road and notice that there is no fork and only *one* road with a sign labeled inexpressible nothingness! We know meaning, whatever it is, lies ahead, but we are hesitant because to continue on means we have to act for ourselves, and we know we will never know if we do. We reflect upon our choices only to realize there is nothing to reflect upon except the meaningless and the lone sign in front of us.'